Stars
above
My Hearse

Michael Tritico

iUniverse, Inc.
Bloomington

Stars above My Hearse

iUniverse books may be ordered through booksellers or by contacting:

iUniverse
1663 Liberty Drive
Bloomington, IN 47403
www.iuniverse.com
1-800-Authors (1-800-288-4677)

ISBN: 978-1-4620-0793-6 (sc)
ISBN: 978-1-4620-0795-0 (dj)
ISBN: 978-1-4620-0794-3 (ebk)

Printed in the United States of America

iUniverse rev. date: 4/6/2011

For All Who Try So Hard
To Change the World for the Better

Contents

Preface

The magnificence of our universe is tarnished by disorder. I do not believe that our Creator meant for turmoil to distract us from the enjoyment of beauty. I do believe that He intends for us to share in the creative processes. First though, we must overcome our personal chaos, our political confusion, and our global violence. It is hard to build symmetry upon a foundation of disarray.

In the mid-1960s our country was experiencing relatively sudden (and definitely unexpected) departures from the docile inertia of the preceding decade. From the highest leadership levels down through the massive bureaucracy and into the family level, things were upset, destabilized. People who had seen a chance to build a more and more just society had inadvertently stimulated resentful backlashes. Furthermore, America had oozed into a war supposedly based upon our need to provide the proven foundations of freedom to the less fortunate people of Asia. Yet the freedoms here seemed to be increasingly suppressed as the tragic costs of the war escalated.

Every home had a new machine, a television, that each evening presented moving eyewitness accounts of what was bad in the world, how people were hurting each other, who was suffering, how, and how much. Fathers and wives, little brothers and cousins, all Americans became witnesses to the real evils that had previously been vague, or not even matters of thought.

Not thinking about things, not talking about things, not doing anything about things became things of the past. Everybody soon had an opinion. Everybody else soon tried to convince each other to come over to the other opinion. Blind stability turned into bloodshot discord.

I was a young man in ultra-conservative Louisiana. My personal situation had become one of disappointment and uncertainty. I saw no reason to stay at home and continue to struggle with the same old things month after month. I had cousins out West who told me to come on out to the mountains, get out of my swamp of depression, just take a break. I saw on the television that strange things were happening out there. I was curious. I decided to go west.

This book is an account of some of what happened before I came back home. I was rejuvenated in many ways and determined to fight against things that had kept us down in Louisiana.

What happened to me out West was miraculous. I was not the only person to whom was given the miracle of that time. Thousands of us together lived through a very short era that was unlike any time that we had experienced before or have experienced since. As happens in any time, imperfections, hardships, and sadnesses occur, but that short era, the mid-through-late sixties, at least in certain places, was a time of love. Love overrode all the negatives: no, of course not at every moment in every place within every person, but yes, much, if not most of the time in most of the places and in most of the people who allowed it to happen.

I want to restore that miracle. It could not have happened without the Creator's blessing. We felt that Great Spirit. We tapped into its energy of love, kindness, mercy, sharing, forgiveness, pervasive love. The Spirit grew within us and we shared it with others and it grew within them.

Some people decided to engineer amplification, cultivation of the Spirit of Love. They actually came up with plans and implemented the plans. However, good people with good plans become targeted by the forces of evil. I hope that by telling you about some of those things that happened to us, you, a new generation with the same curiosities and hopes and need for love, will be better able than we were to withstand the forces of evil. Learn from our discoveries and learn from our mistakes.

I feel certain that the Creator of the Universe is standing by to help you start your own "revolution" to restore the spirit of love. Once you have triggered the revival, be like shepherds, watch carefully, care for the weak, bring them to strength and they too will love. New kinds of beauty will appear. I know that it can happen again. I pray that next time it will be sustained forever. I know that He will not withdraw His blessings when We finally get things right.

Acknowledgements

The Creator of the Universe has left me on this planet far longer than I had anticipated. For many years I could not understand why He did that. Finally, after much prayer, I decided that He was allowing me time to transfer from my mind to others some of what I have experienced. I hope that I am doing that correctly. I thank Him for the chance to do it.

My family has always tolerated my idiosyncrasies, with kindness and love. That has gotten me through times that might have destroyed me. Thank you!

Lately, for this book in particular, I am grateful to my brother Frank for his support.

My sister Mary Jane has done a masterful job of editing, correcting my many errors and bringing the manuscript as nearly up to modern publishing standards as I can understand.

Mary Jane also, along with my friend Bobbie Jean, suggested changes that should help readers bridge gaps that were in the original narrative, gaps that I did not realize a reader, especially one from a later generation, might encounter.

Finally, I want to thank all the actual people who became characters in the book, most of them exactly as they were or a few as fragments of composited characters. I hope that none of you who might recognize yourself or part of yourself in an otherwise not-at-all yourself character will understand that what I am trying to do with this book is what we were trying to do during the "revolution." Just as we did not get everything right back then, I could not get it just right this time. We had to try then. I had to try again. The world still needs to be changed. Just do it!

Chapter 1

Intersecting Dimensions

My friends had all been drafted or had eagerly volunteered to go to Viet Nam. I failed the draft board physical. I was rejected and dejected. The faraway war was becoming inglorious and local. As the first of my friends came home to be buried with full military honors, I saw their families crying. I was too confused to cry.

Louisiana was depressing, so I hitched rides to Reno where I had some cousins. They tolerated me, but after a few weeks of gambling, I realized that my luck at blackjack could not last. I bought an old, round, green Buick with bad shock absorbers. It looked and moved like a turtle, so I called it "The Turtle." I bought a tent and some camping equipment. The Turtle and I hit the road to see real mountains.

As I rounded a curve and looked through a mist into Yosemite Valley for the first time, I was stunned at the surreal beauty that I saw. There were great cliffs with clouds hanging from their bellies, a waterfall that was taller than any building in my hometown of Lake Charles. There was a green, black and tan, yellow, speckled white and brown meadow: the floor of the valley that went for miles below and away from me. I pulled the Turtle into an overlook and we just watched. We watched as the clouds teased each other, as the stream twisted its whitecaps through the meadow beneath the trees way, way down…

At home everything was flat. The only hills were the highway overpasses. Home was two-dimensional but that had seemed normal.

Suddenly, very suddenly, my mind expanded into three dimensions. I wondered whether or not there might be even more dimensions.

No, I told myself, do not be greedy for more than what you have been given so unexpectedly. It will take at least a lifetime to enjoy this new dimension. I woke up the Turtle, and we crawled down the curves to the campground.

There were "Flower Children" there, "Hippies." I'd seen a few along the roads in the past few weeks, but these looked more relaxed, as I was, serene in a newfound place of peace.

Then I thought of my friends in Viet Nam and I felt very guilty.

I began fiddling with the tent, trying to figure out how it went together. A hippie couple came over, holding hands. The girl offered me a bright yellow flower like the millions I'd passed along the roadway. I took it and responded "Thanks. This is really a pretty place, isn't it?"

She smiled and her boyfriend said, "Here's how it goes," and started putting the tent poles together. I thanked him for showing me the way, and we soon had everything done.

"Would you like to get turned on?" he asked. I tried to figure out what he meant but missed it.

I said, "I already am, this place really is mind-boggling!" The couple laughed.

He said, "How long have you been in California?"

"Just today," I replied exuberantly, "What a day!"

"Where did you come from?" the girl asked.

"Louisiana, by way of Reno for a few weeks, both nice places, but I've never seen anything like this place, ever."

"We know what you mean," she said.

The boy said "Listen, some of us are going to walk over to hear the Campfire Naturalist give a talk on ecology just after dark. Would you like to go with us? It will be just on the other side of those trees."

"Yes, I think I'd like that."

The hippie girl said, "Okay, see you after awhile. Peace!" She held her hand up with two fingers spread, making a "V."

"Yes. Peace!" I said back, thinking how little of that my friends overseas must be having, while I was here engorged with it. What is ecology, I thought?

The Turtle had had a long, hard day, climbing thousands of feet, then leaning back against gravity, scraping its claws against the blacktop. I checked its oil and water. It was okay. I patted the top of its shell, "Rest old buddy, just rest, no more work for awhile."

People were lighting their campfires. The smoke smelled sweet, different from the marsh fires and pine smokes back home. The other scents, from the forest and cascading waters, were fresh, crisp and pleasant, without the hints of mildew or sulfur that drifted out of our swamps, especially in the summer. There were no mosquitoes.

I did not build a campfire. I opened a can of Spam and ate it on white bread with some mustard. As I was finishing that, the hippies came along, singing, "Will you still love me when I'm sixty-four?" Nice thought, I thought; who says the kids these days have no thought for the future?

"Pretty song," I said.

"You've never heard it before?" one of the girls asked.

"No, I haven't."

"It's by the Beatles."

"Beatles?" I asked.

"Yes, they are from England. You need to hear their new album."

"Well, I guess I'll have to listen for them on the radio, no record players in the tent or the Turtle." I pointed to my car.

"Oh--Wow! Yes! It is a Turtle. It is! A giant flying Turtle, like the Sopwith Camel!"

I was puzzled. I knew that a Sopwith Camel had been a World War One British fighting biplane. The girl continued raving on, "Yes, the Sopwith Turtle! Right here in the Valley. The Sopwith Turtle!" I looked at the original hippie couple.

They were grinning. "She's really having a good trip!"

I said courteously, "Yes, so am I; it just keeps getting more and more interesting."

They laughed. "Just wait, it's going to be so much better for you, you just cannot imagine!"

These kids are weird, I thought, but a happy weird, and that's good, that's very good.

"Come on, let's go hear Ranger Rick's talk on Yosemite lizard ecology. Last night he told us about the rocks, this one should be more wiggly at least!" the girl danced.

The original hippie girl had noticed my empty can of Spam. She seemed to revert into some kind of maternal mode and chided me: "You really need to eat real food, tomorrow you come eat with us, okay?"

"Okay," I muttered, thinking that it would be hard to think that Spam was imaginary and what could be more real than mustard.

I told them that my name was Mike. The girl was Sara and the boy was Bob. Their little giggly, wiggly blue-eyed friend had huge blonde Afro-style hair. I never learned her real name. My friends and I later always just called her "Jolie Blonde."

We got to the Naturalist's campfire. It was in front of a little primitive amphitheater. He was talking to people as they gathered. Some were old people, some were perfect American families with well-behaved children of stair step heights. There were flower children and even two Hell's Angels that sat on the back row like chaperones.

The Ranger-Naturalist introduced himself and led us in the Pledge of Allegiance. Then he asked who would like to lead the singing. "No, you have to do it like last night! That's your job, remember!" one middle-aged woman hollered and everybody cheered.

The Naturalist faked a terrible groan and protested, "You know I cannot sing, why punish me, why make me punish all these first-timers?"

"Sing! Sing! Sing!" they began to chant.

He yodeled a truly awful "You are my Sunshine! My only Sunshine!" and they all screamed and laughed and I thought: That song was written by Jimmie Davis; it made him governor of Louisiana, maybe it'll do something similar for this guy. We need somebody with a sense of humor, even if he truly cannot sing... terrible, terrible singing.

However, the crowd had mercy and began singing along and over the Ranger, beautifully, and he grinned and conducted like that famous guy from the Boston Pops. After a few songs ending with "America the Beautiful," we heard a simple but great account of reptile ecology and I learned what the word ecology meant: interrelationships, interconnectedness of everything, one life dependent upon another and upon the death of another for new life, eternal order from disorder, peace from conflict, love from hate – no, the animals do not hate, only evil hates.

The Naturalist did not get that far in his talk, it just came to me going beyond the end of his progression along the concepts of ecology. Remarkable, I thought, I wonder if the Park Service trained this guy to work our minds like this, or maybe it's just his personal gift. Fascinating, no wonder the hippies, the families, the old people, and even the Hell's Angels came tonight. No wonder he was so self-deprecating about the singing, just to gain a chance for commonality with the people. I thought about some of the special teachers from my early life, how they could "educate" me beyond the facts, expand my thinking for years afterward, just by having triggered my mind's release, then having oriented it toward new truths.

As we walked back in the moonlight, the hippies began to sing another song they said was from the Beatles new album. The song was "Eleanor Rigby."

"How sad," I thought, "I guess there was some element of reality in the Ranger's talk that has made them more somber."

"No, let's sing White Rabbit!" They shifted into a different, odd mode, Alice in Wonderland. We got back to my camp and as the group kept going and singing, I asked if that were also a Beatles song. "No, one of our local groups, Great Society. See you in the morning!"

Wonderland, yes. I was in Wonderland. I let my mind leave behind the sadnesses of home. I told the Sopwith Turtle goodnight and had a wonderland sleep.

Chapter 2

Marin County

Bob and Sara woke me up for breakfast. It was something called granola, a homemade kind of cereal. It was okay, but the goat's milk part of it I could have done without. I did not tell them that.

Bob said that he was majoring in visual arts. His dad had been a pioneer of art in comic books. I was surprised that I was actually talking with someone who knew the inventor of one of my longtime action heroes.

Bob said "We just found out last night that the Charlatans, Janis and Big Brother are going to be at the Avalon tonight, so we are going to leave right away. Want to come with us?"

I figured out that they were talking about some musicians, so I asked, "Where?"

"Oh, San Francisco. We will go home first, Mill Valley, pick up some more friends, then back across the bridge to the Avalon. While we are home you can listen to Sergeant Pepper, that's the Beatles new album."

"How long a trip is it and maybe I should take the Turtle, I don't want to put y'all out."

"No, no problem, plenty of room in the van, and we're going to get the pickup at home. It'll be nice for some of us to ride in the back on the way into town tonight."

"Well, when are you coming back here? Where would I stay tonight?"

Sara laughed. "You'll never have to worry about where to crash. Everybody stays wherever they happen to be. It'll be okay."

That bothered me, a lot, but Sara seemed so happy and so innocent that I concluded that the Guardian Angels must be protecting her and everyone around her. Her sparkly-eyes chipped away my resistance. She seemed certain of things and her childlike confidence shamed me into taking the risk.

"So be it, " I said. "The Avalon, how much does it cost to get in?"

"Sara takes up the tickets when the other girl goes on break. Be ready in about half an hour," Bob instructed. He was tall and moved like Batman.

I really did not want to leave Yosemite so soon, or the Turtle, but I sensed an adventure.

In the van the hippies were jubilant, talking about things that seemed disconnected at times and then profoundly insightful at other times. Jolie Blonde and a couple of teenaged boys were in the back talking about Ranger Rick's lizards and some artist named Escher and how they were going to have to go back to the Art Institute and look at them again. Sara said she was looking forward to the Klee exhibit. I knew so little about art that I felt helplessly left out of the conversation. Sara, always sensitive to what others were feeling, noticed my mental discomfort and began giving me a guided tour of the little towns and gold-panning streams along the way.

"How do you know so much about this area?" I asked.

"Bob and I grew up in the Bay Area, but we get our water from up here, the Hetch Hetchy Reservoir. Every summer our families reserved two weeks at Camp Mather, the special enclave beside Yosemite. The camp is for citizens of the Bay Area; sort of grandfathered in from when the park was being created and then the aqueduct. Camp Mather's where Bob and I met, as children; we love it up here and we love it back in Marin County."

"Marin County, I take it, is somewhat on the outskirts of San Francisco?" I asked.

"Yes, just north of the city, across the Golden Gate Bridge. Marin is mostly residential. The City has the businesses and museums and all, but Marin is quieter and very beautiful."

As we got down from the mountains into a hot valley, I noticed flat fields of different crops, some with orchard trees, some with vineyards, and some with vegetables. There were groups of people stooped over the vegetables, harvesting them. "That looks like very hard work," I said.

"Yes," Bob said. "The poor Mexicans come up here because they have no jobs at home. A man named Cesar Chavez has been trying to get better pay for them and toilets and places to live, but some people say he is a radical Communist."

Jolie Blonde piped up from the back "Yeah, they say that about us, too! What's a Communist anyway?" and she giggled and went back to her teenaged boys.

I thought about the required courses back home in Louisiana: Americanism vs. Communism, Civics, American Government, and wondered whether or not such courses were missing from the California schools.

Sara said, "There are definitely some serious problems in this country. Like the war. We are just going to have to do something about it all."

I thought: "What can we do, the world controls us, we don't control the world. People invade our friends and we defend them and try to establish democracy. We grow more crops than we can pick so we let other people come pick for us." I had not left in the flatland all the conflicts that kept me uptight. Back home machines had replaced the field workers except at the prisons. Seeing the Mexicans laboring in California reminded me of scenes from my childhood, seeing forlorn groups of people picking cotton out in the mud and hot sun.

Still, I remembered my father coming back from World War II talking about how good all people in the United States have it compared to the people he saw overseas and how we should find a way to help those people. He made me pray on my knees every night for the poor people in China, Burma, and India.

We got into the Bay Area and traffic. "Yes, this is a city, definitely," I thought, "just where I do not need to be."

Sara again noticed my tension. "Don't worry, we'll soon be home." We went up and down city hills so steep that I was definitely glad I had not brought the Turtle. I made up my mind never to do it, not to San Francisco. The thought of having to drive on such nearly vertical inclined planes was frightening.

The architecture was very interesting, old Victorian-style buildings but tall, three or four stories high, with bay windows all the way up.

"Oh," I realized, "maybe that is why they are called bay windows, because people look out from them and see San Francisco Bay."

It was late afternoon when we reached the south end of a magnificent structure, the Golden Gate Bridge. I'd seen it in movies, but I had not realized how large it is, how beyond human daring. Who could have had the arrogance to believe it could be brought to reality? Maybe it was not arrogance but divine guidance. Anything that intricate and massive has to be at least allowed by the Creator. We seemed to cross it too quickly; I felt that I needed more time to absorb the bridge's spirit, like the unique spirit of Yosemite that I felt already being shoved aside. I was getting to and leaving places too quickly. I was being introduced to the pace of California.

Mill Valley was a neat little place up and down and around damp forested curves. "This is a different kind of rain forest from what we have at home," I thought, "more like a fog forest, very pretty." We dropped off Jolie Blonde and her boys.

"Eight o'clock more or less," waved Sara as we drove off.

"Mike, here's my dad's place. He's in Europe. Come in and I'll set you up with Sergeant Pepper. Then Sara and I are going over to her place to make some calls and get ready. We'll be back for you around eight o'clock, more or less."

Bob's dad's place was hanging on the side of a hill. I could not see how it was hung there and I felt strangely uncomfortable waiting for it to fall down carrying me with it in an avalanche of timbers through the trees and houses that were hanging below us then back down to the bottom. I quit looking at that vertical anomaly (relative to Louisiana's coastal plain) when Bob cranked up the album. The first few notes... "It was twenty years ago, today..." There was a strange framework in the song. So much for Conway Twitty...

Bob saw the look on my face and laughed. "Enjoy, we'll be back soon."

Bob was back with a pickup truck, too soon. I wanted to play the album over again.

"Okay, Mike, ready for the next level?"

Adventure was happening, no doubt. I was surrendering to who knew what, but it felt safe.

"Yes. I'm ready. What's next?'

"Getting turned on." Bob pulled out some hand-rolled cigarettes.

"I don't smoke," I said, knowing that it was not tobacco but probably that reefer stuff I'd been warned against.

"This is marijuana. A joint will help you enjoy the concert; it won't hurt you."

"Isn't it illegal?" I asked, knowing the answer, of course.

"Well, around here that law is not enforced because many of the people who govern the place get stoned too, even some of the police. One of our friends is called Sergeant Sunshine; we might see him tonight at the Avalon. We'll smoke a joint with him if you like, so you can relax about it."

Smoking an illegal substance with a cop was not a relaxing thought. Still, sensing a reversion to my depressing thoughts about the real tyrannies of home, I chose to surrender in optimism instead to the new unknowns. Bob lit the cigarette.

"Breathe it in and hold it in, like this."

I did and handed it back to him. Nothing happened. I exhaled. We handed it back and forth a few times and Bob said "Let's go, got to pick up some more friends. Sara's already headed over to the Avalon."

We maneuvered around and down some curves to another beautiful hillside home.

"Here, you sit in the back with my friends. They are musicians, like from Brementown," and he told me their names which I've forgotten. Years later I realized, I think, but cannot be sure, that they were to become well-known as a musical group named: no, I can't be sure, best not to say. A beautiful day became a beautiful evening.

In the back of the pickup truck Bob's friends lit a jumbo joint. We passed it around. As we got to the Golden Gate Bridge I began to notice some strange feelings or sensations or something I could not put my finger on, just something different. The lights on the bridge seemed to pass in a rhythm that was getting stretched out. I was able to begin absorbing the spirit of the bridge, and I gave thanks for the bonus. We passed under one of the great, tall towers that held up the cables. It seemed to be a ladder to heaven. Time passed and the lights moved by seemingly more and more slowly even though the truck was chugging its same cadence. The cables arched down toward me, and I felt as though I were in a cradle as they arched slowly, slowly back upward. The next tower laddered its way up into a cloud. Then the cables came slowly back out of the golden, reflected mist and the lights passed even more slowly. Ladders for giants...

I was absorbing the spirit of more than the bridge. One of the musicians asked, "What do you think, Mike?"

I shook my head, "I cannot think, it is just incredible, absolutely beautiful and awesome."

"Yes, awesome."

We got to the Avalon and must have parked somewhere, I cannot remember that. We stood around outside for a few minutes enjoying the mist until Bob motioned for us to come in. Sara passed us through into a big darkened room, rather, a small ballroom. I could see that there was a stage at one end. There were dozens of people inside already, and some were smoking. One group had a hookah.

There were two or three areas along the walls with ultraviolet lights. Hippies were painting on the walls and floors with glow-in-the-dark paints of different colors. I passed one of the spots and saw some gorgeous, intricate animals, some geometric designs that seemed to repeat at larger and smaller scales, and also some things that just looked like random splashes and lines.

A group of musicians were on the stage arranging their apparatus. They began what started to sound like tuning up but the sounds developed into an acoustic scaffold which they repeated in different keys back and forth for a few minutes until a slightly chubby girl with messed up hair came on stage and people started clapping and whistling and yelling, "Hey, Janis! Do it!" She did. I'd grown up hearing black people sing blues, but she was the first white girl I'd ever seen or heard who could nail it. I smiled. "Where did she come from?" I wondered. I found out later that she'd come from just over the border from Lake Charles, Port Arthur. Her high school and mine had even played football against each other. Maybe I'd seen her across the field. Never like I saw her that night, though--she hammered it into us.

About midway into her first song, some lights came on from around the balcony projected onto the ceiling. I'd never seen anything like that, either. There were pools of color within pools of color, blue drops and bubbles inside yellow bubbles and drops, red swirls inside purple swirls, and green globs around pink globs all moving in time with the music, perfectly, no matter how the music changed, no matter how the drops and globs changed, colors perfectly in time and in tune with the music. I felt that I must have been approaching sensory saturation yet there was more and more room for more and more.

Someone by the wall flipped on a brilliant flashing strobe light which was also in perfect time with the music and a hippie girl began twirling a long set of beads under the light. The beads seemed frozen in space then slowly rotated first in one direction and then back, while she was twirling them fast and then slowly and then fast again, yet everything stayed constantly synchronized with the music. I understood "mind blown."

Why is this stuff illegal, I thought? It is obviously a gift from the Creator, like a great flavor or pleasant odor or an inspiring sunset. This stuff could... change the world... make people appreciate peace... and each other... So, why is it illegal?

A very disconcerting thought occurred to me, one that I would occasionally confide to people I knew to have heard the story in the Bible about the fall of mankind. There was a plant that Adam and Eve were not supposed to sample, the Tree of Knowledge of Good and Evil. The Deceiver told them that it would be okay for them to eat from that tree because in that day they would be like God, able to know all that is right from all that is wrong. As the marijuana clarified my mind, letting me see new facets of reality, I wondered whether or not I had inadvertently made mankind's original mistake.

After Big Brother and the Holding Company and Janis finished, there was a short break and then another group was to perform. Between those sets Bob introduced me to Perry.

"Mike, I want you to meet Perry. His grandfather designed that bridge we came over awhile ago. Perry also lives in Yosemite when he isn't down here."

Perry looked a little older than the other hippies. He was about my age. He had light, sandy hair, a full handlebar mustache, penetrating blue eyes, a wide grin, beads, a tie-died shirt, blue paisley pants, and sandals. He was very neat but very unconventional looking.

"Hello, Perry, I'm glad to meet you. That bridge is incredible."

"Yes, we all have bridges to build, some more challenging than others."

I sensed a challenge to me in what he said as if he had been challenged by his grandfather's accomplishment, had accepted the challenge, and wanted to share the conquest. I wondered what Bob and Sara had told him about me. It seemed like I was being drawn into something more than just beautiful sights and sounds.

"What could be more challenging than the bridge your grandfather built?"

"Love in this time of trouble, peace in this time of conflict, justice in this time of unfairness, getting power back to the people..."

Normally, that would have sounded like sophomoric gobbledygook, but when Perry said it there was a depth of longing that was anchored in his utter sincerity.

"Yes, those would be more challenging if not impossible," I answered.

"No, not impossible, very possible. You and I must talk about this in Yosemite. Bob says you will be staying there for awhile." Yes, I guessed, yes, I would, for awhile; I would stay.

A group called The Charlatans began to play, more bizarre order, rhythm, lights, melody, sensations, moods, thoughts, synchronizations... amazing... synchronizations...I would stay.

Chapter 3

Fire Control

As the Avalon closed for the night, we stepped out into the San Francisco chill. Perry suggested that I ride back to Yosemite with him since Bob and Sara had decided to stay in the Bay Area for a few days. I accepted that invitation, told Bob and Sara how much I'd enjoyed the entire experience and that I looked forward to seeing them back up in the mountains.

Perry and I talked as we walked the deserted streets to his apartment. I saw in him a strange mixture of dreamer, pragmatist, advocate, activist, pacifist, philosopher, skeptic, cynic, and planner. He was inordinately intelligent, gentle, angry, determined to change the world using love and whatever else it took, having faith that love was the primary weapon.

"When we get to my apartment you will meet Zack and Jim. They work for the Park Service in Yosemite. They are Fire Control Aides. Tonight they went to the other concert, at the Fillmore."

"What's a Fire Control Aide?"

"They do controlled burns to try to mimic the old natural pattern of fires that kept too much fuel from accumulating on the floor of the forest. When some fire goes through a place with too much fuel and starts damaging the living trees, they suppress the fire. Sometimes they bust the Forest Service firemen for racing through Yosemite on the way to put out fires on adjacent Forest Service land."

"What?" I asked, thinking I'd misunderstood something.

Perry laughed. "Yeah, there is a big difference of opinion between Park Service and Forest Service. Forest Service thinks they have to prevent and stop all fires, but that is what lets the duff build up to unnatural levels and leads to catastrophic heat when a fire passes through. The Park Service Naturalists are trying to reestablish a natural equilibrium. There is a speed limit in the Park. Zack and Jim love to chase down the Forest Service firetrucks with their firetruck. It's about the only time they get to use their siren. When they catch the Forest Service guys and pull them over, the tourists get quite a show. Jim plays 'bad cop.' He's from Nebraska. Zack plays 'good cop.' He's from San Mateo, runs his own chapter of the Sexual Freedom League."

I was beginning to wish I'd stayed with Bob and Sara.

Perry's apartment was in an old Victorian building. Zack and Jim were not yet there. Perry had an odd mixture of posters, paintings, and radical newspapers thumbtacked neatly on the walls. "Those are nice paintings," I said.

"Yes, my friend Elena does them. She also writes for Cesar Chavez' newsletters. Her ancestors were some of the Spanish aristocrats way back when the missions were built. You'll meet her in Wawona. She works at the hotel there during the summer season."

"Where's Wawona?"

"It's in the southern part of Yosemite. That's where my home is. My brother Tim and I live there most of the time. Our mother still has the family home in Sausalito but I keep this place in the City for logistical reasons."

"You have a home within the park boundaries?"

"Yes, our grandfather built it back when the park was just in the planning stages. So, we were literally 'grandfathered-in' like a few other families surrounded by public lands. We've always had the option to sell to the Park Service, but that's not going to happen."

"I should guess not, you had a very wise grandfather."

"Yes, he was special. So's Tim. He's a grad student at UC Berkeley, one of those crazy 'radical revolutionaries' you've heard about no doubt," and he sort of winked to let me know that I should not be seriously worried about brother Tim.

We heard some rowdies getting out of a car downstairs. "They're here," said Perry.

As they plodded up the stairs, Zack and Jim and Tim were singing something about a "White Room."

Perry said, "They went to hear 'Cream,' an English group. Sort of neurotic, high energy, more like Los Angeles music than Bay Area. Good musicians, though."

Perry opened the door and in came a short, frail-looking, sandy-haired fellow. Perry introduced us: "This is Zack, and this is Jim." Jim was tall, scrawny, but dangerous-looking. "This is Mike, he's new, from Louisiana. Bob and Sara turned him on tonight, took him to the Avalon. He'll be going back up to Yosemite with us."

Zack cheered, "Ho! New Orleens, eh? What a place!"

"No," I said unapologetically. "Actually I'm from higher ground, Lake Charles, near Texas." Zack looked disappointed.

Jim said "Glad to meet you, I'm from Nebraska, we grow corn and weed, all you need."

"Glad to meet both of you. Perry tells me you chase down fire trucks with your fire truck. I'd love to see that!'

"Stick with us and you'll see things so unreal you'll have to believe!" Jim charmed.

Perry went on with the introductions, "And this is my brother, Tim, the thinker."

We were glad to meet each other.

I was picking up mostly good spirits from Zack and Jim and Tim, so I began to relax again. Perry lit a joint. It got shorter and shorter as it made the rounds. Jim taught me how to use just my thumb to pass the "roach" along to the next person.

Zack suggested that Perry put the "demo" on the stereo. It was an odd-sized vinyl record. "Some of our friends: Country Joe and the Fish. Give us your honest opinion." The song was "Martha Lorraine" who was going to "sit by my bedside and watch me die." I was thoroughly bewildered by the words. The music was a form of cosmic order that I'd never encountered, order so extreme that it was startling. It was as though the Creator Himself had said, "Let there be music," and "it was good," but the worry about the Tree of Knowledge of Good and Evil returned. I realized they were all quietly looking at me, waiting for my critique. I could not speak. I looked from one to the other and shook my head in awe. They simultaneously burst out laughing. The singer shifted the song's architecture and said "Too bad you never learned nothing about country ways...about country ways..." I was comforted, partly. I wondered what country part of America had spawned that singer. If he could absorb and adapt, I figured, so could I.

Next morning we went down to Zack's car, an old white Chevrolet. He patted the trunk like I would pat the Turtle, then opened it up so they could throw in their duffel bags. They all looked around snickering at me, like mischievous boys on a schoolyard. "Did you see that?" Jim asked me.

"I saw it. Is it what I think it is?"

"Yeah, about two weeks' supply."

It was about ten bricks of marijuana, about a kilo or two pounds each.

"Y'all can't possibly smoke that much in two weeks," I said.

"No, Yosemite... the hotel workers, naturalists, trail crew, tourists, this will hold everybody for a couple of weeks until our next days off."

Perry said, "It's part of the Plan. We started with Yosemite and the Bay Area and now we've added L.A., Laguna Beach, Monterey, Mendocino, and Oregon. Let's get rolling, no pun intended."

I was uncomfortable again, riding with a big load of illegal substance. I kept running through my mind what I would tell the cops: "I didn't know it was there. It's not mine. I just met these guys. Are you kidding, marijuana? I'm just hitching a ride." I knew that there was no escape. I was surely trapped. If we were to get caught...

My friend Alain from Louisiana was somewhere out here as a fugitive because he got caught at home with two joints and was convicted and sentenced to thirty years. Now I was facing at least several lifetimes in prison. I was very uncomfortable.

Zack was driving carefully at least. Jim was rolling a joint. Perry and I were in the back seat.

Perry said "You look nervous. Don't be. We do this all the time." Doing... Time...

"No, thanks, I don't feel like it right now," I said and Jim passed the joint over to Perry.

Zack said "He'll be okay once we get out of the city, eh, Mike?"

"Yeah, I guess. I just keep thinking about..." and I told them Alain's story.

"Bummer" said Jim. "Do you know where he is? We could probably set up some cover for him."

"No, I just heard that he was out here somewhere, I'm sure he is just scared to death, probably holed up in somebody's remote cabin or ghetto apartment, I just have no idea."

"Bummer," said Zack.

Perry seemed pensive. "It sounds like Louisiana needs some help."

"Yeah," I murmured. "I love the place but we've never gotten past Reconstruction, you know, the carpetbaggers coming in with papers letting them take over all the resources and power, and the scalawags, those hometown hustlers that figure out how to beg riches from the carpetbaggers while selling out their own families sometimes. And then, there's New Orleans, below sea level, just waiting for the next drownings. I was there in Betsy, 90 people died. Yeah, Louisiana has problems, plenty of problems."

Tim asked "What's Betsy, a hurricane?"

"Yes, a couple of years ago. Before that I was in Audrey, 1957; 500 people died just south of Lake Charles including my aunt, and not counting who knows how many hundreds of Negroes. They were menhaden fishermen from North Carolina in Cameron for the harvest season, not on our official census records."

Zack said "Well, here we've got earthquakes. You just have to roll with the punches."

"No, I think we should use our common sense and learn where to live and not where to live, like the animals learn," I argued.

"In Nebraska we have tornadoes, but we also have storm cellars."

"In Yosemite we have heaven," bragged Perry, "just have to not fall off its cliffs like Lucifer."

I was glad I'd not smoked anything since I was still stoned from the night before. These guys are fascinating, I thought.

I asked "Perry, you talked about a Plan that you started in the Bay Area and in Yosemite. What kind of Plan are you talking about, turning everybody on with marijuana?"

"No, revolution, a restoration of love. Grass is just one of the tools. It helps people see things they would normally overlook or run past so fast that they would miss the significance. The Plan is to sow love to expand people's minds so that we humans can stop destroying ourselves and our planet with war, greed, all sorts of injustice. As people come to appreciate truth they will necessarily become more loving and kind, and the love and kindness and truth will be contagious."

Tim added "We just have to plant enough seeds in enough places to generate enough of a harvest to tip things back in a sane direction. When the people get it, the politicians will have to turn around. We just have to highlight the truths and put spotlights on the hypocrisies and show everyone as much love as we can..."

The most fascinating thing about what Perry and Tim were saying was that they believed it. I did not want to discourage them. "That is a very noble and ambitious Plan. It would be nice if it could work."

"It is working." "Yes, very much so." "Definitely." "On its way." They each believed.

I thought, "No way, not at home, too many scalawags, double-crossers, too many trusting good people who don't want to look at the bad things, who would rather wink at a funny crook than try to get him out of office--no way, not at home."

"Tell me this," I asked. "Do you adopt every stranger you run across, and indoctrinate us with your Plan?"

There was a short silence, then Perry said, "Actually, no, Mike. We do show everyone kindness and try to get them thinking a little but, but some, like you, we bring in deeper."

"Why?"

"Frankly, we see that some strong people are either more off in a wrong direction or that they are just unaware of things but either way, if we can get them to see things the way we see them, such people will become powerful allies, powerful advocates for truth, peace, and love."

"Makes sense. I hope you don't think I am too far off in a wrong direction just because I come from a Southern state."

"No, you seem to be pretty level-headed."

"I try to be. My father was a historian and political scientist. I studied the same kinds of things until I dropped out of college last year, too tedious."

"Yeah, tedious," said Jim.

Several hours and mind-bending discussions later we approached Yosemite but Zack turned off onto a narrow, gravel road that wound upward on increasingly-steeper hairpin curves. We got to a steel gate. Jim jumped out and opened the padlock with a key. "Here we are, home again, men!" He locked the gate behind us and got back into the car.

Soon we took yet another side road, even narrower and steeper. At the top we got out of the car. Zack took a kilo out of the trunk and we hiked up another quarter of a mile to a fire lookout tower. Bernie, the lookout, was down at the bottom of the tower waiting for us. Zack handed him the kilo. Bernie said "The guys have been getting antsy, especially Snap Bean, about to snap again. They'll be glad to get this."

Jim asked in a serious tone, "Everything clear?"

Bernie said "Yep, nothing happening."

Zack patted him on the back, "Good man, Bernie, just let us know."

"Okay, and thanks, all of you, thanks from all of us."

"Sure thing, no problem."

We got back into the car and meandered very carefully down the mountain. Nobody was talking. I sensed a somber mood, but I did not ask. It seemed that something deep was on their minds.

Perry finally said, "That war has got to be stopped. Fast." I wondered what Viet Nam had to do with Bernie and the lookout tower.

"Well, we've got 'em along this far, it's just that we can't handle many more; or it'll self-destruct," said Zack.

Jim said "I'd better talk to Stan again. If I can get him to set up another location, in the Tuolumne Meadows area, then we wouldn't have to add any more to this crew. It is at a limit, too precarious."

"But you know he's not going to turn any of them away, he can't," said Perry.

"How are you going to convince him we're saturated?" asked Zack.

I finally asked "What are y'all talking about?"

Perry said, "When they get back from Nam, some of the men can't readjust to America. They've changed and America's changed. It's dynamite. Some of them go stark raving crazy and hurt themselves or whoever happens to be next to them. Some of them go catatonic and just get parked in a VA ward, indefinitely, endlessly."

Jim said, "One of the rangers here, Stan Kelly, is trying an experiment in conjunction with the VA. He's set up a trail crew out in the back country away from anybody but Park Service and the Sierra Club hikers and the few other people who trickle back there. The trail crew all have Viet Nam in common. They all have in common a desire to go back to their pre-war lives. They all know that they would not be able to make it, not yet."

Zack said, "So, they all spend the days working hard with pickaxes and shovels, building new trails, repairing old trails, and thinking. They help us with fire control projects. In the evenings they have campfires and try to forget the days of having to worry if the noise of urinating onto the jungle floor would be enough to alert the enemy to their location. At night they try to sleep having an ax by their sides instead of a gun. This is our first crew and it has been touchy, but we think it is working."

Perry said "We leave them alone, mostly. They know that only a very few of us know their situation. Zack, Jim, Bernie, and Stan are their official contacts. I'm the interface for their weed and for anything that might come up between them and the flower children. They've already learned not to worry about us. They have more trouble with some of the Sierra Club people, who sort of think they own the park since John Muir had a lot to do with starting both the park and the Club. Anyway, these are very strong men who hate war."

Tim mused "They will be the most powerful voices against it when they are ready to speak publicly. I would not be surprised to see one of them become president someday."

How many irons do these guys have in the fire, I wondered? What would the average American think if he knew what was going on out here in California? What if Perry's Plan actually did spread it to the rest of the country? What would happen? Maybe they could stop the war. Maybe we could get rid of some scalawags. No, not likely, not back home; not without at least another forty years of wandering around in Louisiana's political wilderness.

Nevertheless, I felt proud that the real spirit of America, unity with liberty and justice for all, was actually being exercised somewhere during a time of conflict. It was being utilized in a real way by real people who might have chosen to be adversaries but who instead respected each other for being able to think in truth, as individuals. Warriors and revolutionaries, all dedicated to the pursuit of happiness, loving each other... I saw that there could again be a happy America.

Chapter 4

South Yosemite

After leaving the lookout we made a quick delivery at a tent cabin area where some park employees lived. Perry said he'd introduce me to them later. At the Wawona Hotel he brought Elena out to meet me. She was beautiful. "Out of my league," I instantly realized. Too bad, it was one of those "love-at-first-sight" moments I get every few years. It seemed strange that such a gorgeous young lady was dressed in a menial worker's uniform. In Louisiana she probably would have been colored.

My mind, I thought, things are getting upside down. In Louisiana she would be... the rich, spoiled brat.

"Mike, Mike, this is Elena."

"Hello, Mike. Perry tells me that Bob and Sara showed you the migrant workers down in the valley."

I sensed that she was aware of my awe, my automatic reaction to her beauty. The fact that she immediately closed that door and opened a different door reinforced my instinct to suppress the "love-at-first-sight" syndrome.

"Yes," I said. "It reminded me of home, especially the convicts, the field hands at the Angola Prison. Only differences I saw were no stripes on the clothes and no men on horseback with shotguns."

"Well, things are not as obvious, maybe, but don't kid yourself, it is still a kind of imprisonment. How is it that you've seen the convicts at Angola?" Elena asked. "We've heard the Leadbelly songs, but we thought that particular prison was kept pretty much out of the public eye."

"That's true, but one of my father's professors from LSU got taken down in a political purge after Huey Long was assassinated. The warden let the professor be kind of a butler in the mansion. We would go visit once a year, and the professor would drive us around the prison to see the levees and the prisoners out in the hot sun. Daddy figured it was a good deterrent; that I was not likely to grow up doing things that would land me in prison. It worked..." (and then I thought... "up to now").

Perry broke in, "Okay, Elena, we've got to make a few more stops. Come by the house tonight if you can."

"Thanks, Perry. Everyone says tell you thanks, this means a lot to us," and she folded the package up in her apron.

I was curious, so, back in the car, I came right out and asked. "I've heard that marijuana is expensive but nobody is paying you for it."

Zack and Jim looked a little nervous. Jim said, "Sounds like a cop question. Are you a cop, Mike?"

"No, oh, no, I just can't keep up with everything that is going on."

Perry said, "Well, we all have to trust each other if we are going to get any good done. I am just going to trust you, Mike, like Zack trusts me and Jim trusts Zack and Elena trusts Bernie, we all just trust each other and it works."

I said "I'm sorry, I did not mean to create tension."

Zack said "It's okay. A cop would probably not have asked the question aloud, but would have waited to see how it works. How it works is that we give it away. No money passes hands, no sales, no criminal enterprise."

This time I did not ask, but Perry anticipated the question. "Naturally, the growers are in it partly for the money but think of it this way: Some patrons of the arts, like the ones that supported sculptors and poets in the past, support us now. Wealthy little old ladies who hate what war has done to their families' lives, or affluent celebrities whose politics differ from the entrenched cadre of what you would call national-level scalawags, or just hundreds of people throwing in a little bit each for the cause at rallies or concerts... the money is there in the background where it belongs, for now. Someday it won't be necessary at all."

I dared not to ask how Perry became a bridge between or among all the elements of the Plan and its implementations.

Zack dropped Jim off at their tent cabin area along with most of the remaining load.

Perry's home in the Wawona forest was an architecturally-perfect insertion of an unobtrusive human object into a wilderness. The same grandfather that had accomplished the huge, bold bridge across the Golden Gate had also mastered the subtle, minimalist placement of mankind into a sensitive ecosystem. Maybe the man had personally known John Muir.

"Amazing, Perry. How beautiful and balanced."

"Yes. It can be done."

Zack handed Perry the remaining kilos and said "See you tomorrow, peace," and he flashed two fingers in the V shape.

"Peace, " said Perry. They looked at me and I, for the first time, flashed the Peace sign. "Peace."

Zack smiled and drove off.

"Have you seen the Big Trees yet?" Perry asked. I had not. "Tomorrow, we'll hitch a ride up there."

"Maybe I should get back to my camp in Yosemite Valley, check on the Turtle."

"The Turtle?" Perry asked.

"My old car. It looks and rides like a turtle."

"Oh, it'll be okay. We'll get you there in a day or two."

Next morning Perry grabbed his knapsack, and we walked down the rocky creek to the hotel. In the coffee shop Elena was pulling her shift as a waitress. "What can I get for you fellows?"

"I'd like some coffee and a donut," I said.

"Just coffee for me," Perry said.

She brought our breakfast. "Where are you going to take him?" she asked Perry.

"The Big Trees. I think this is Betty's day in the museum up there."

"Oh, good idea. You'll like Betty, Mike. She's a very cool naturalist."

I said, "I got to hear a naturalist the other night, with Bob and Sara, in Yosemite Valley. He was talking about ecology, how lizards are part of it all; it was very interesting."

"That was probably Rick; did he try to sing?" she asked.

"Yes, it was very funny. He's really a terrible singer."

"It's likely an act, you know. He can probably sing as well as Dean Martin," and I detected a note of sarcasm in Elena's voice.

Perry laughed, "Yeah, probably so" and I detected a little more sarcasm.

I thought that Dean Martin could sing just fine, but maybe California tastes were a little different.

We finished our breakfast and stepped out onto the road. Within two minutes a hippie van stopped to give us a ride. They took us as far as the fork in the road that led out of the park down to Fresno where they were headed. Perry gave the driver a small plastic bag of marijuana. Again, in only a couple of minutes we had a ride up toward the Big Trees. I could see why Perry did not bother having a car, no need when so many people were so friendly and so eager to help. Again, when we arrived, Perry gave the driver a bag of marijuana. "Thanks for the lid, man!"

"Thanks for helping us make our trip!" said Perry, and I recognized a phrase from one of the Country Joe and the Fish songs. Perry was always automatically reinforcing any element that appeared anywhere else in what nowadays would be called self-similarity within a fractal universe. Anything that would help remind someone of some other aspect of the "revolution" that was underway got repeated at any appropriate time.

At the Big Trees museum a lady in a Smokey the Bear uniform was giving a talk about the Sequoia trees. We caught the last part of the talk and then Perry introduced me to Betty. "This whole ecology thing is her fault," Perry chided.

Betty blushed. "No, don't start that again, Perry."

"Seriously, Mike, Betty and the other Rangers in Glacier Park, Montana, a couple of years ago, did something monumental, just nobody knows about it. Tell him, Betty."

"All we did was to decide to use the word 'ecology' in each and every conversation we had with any tourist or hotel worker or bus driver or anybody we came in contact with. Then, they would usually ask what it meant and we would give them the simple definition: the interconnectedness of everything, how one thing is linked to another, how huckleberries help the bears, how the bears help the soil, how the soil helps the river and the otters and the gulls... just everything is helping each other, so we should not mess up any part of it."

Perry probed, "And after a year of that, what happened, Betty?"

"People began beating us to the punch, asking about ecology of glacier lilies, marmots, even deer flies. We were quite pleasantly surprised."

"So, now it has become sort of an unofficial directive. Across all the National Parks the Naturalists are lighting the ecology fuse nationwide, right?" prodded Perry.

"Yes, they transferred some of us around to help spread the concept. It's fun to see something take off like it has."

"See, Mike? One just has to have a dream and faith and just do it! Plant seeds and they grow."   I wanted to believe that Perry was right. Betty's account of what she and the Glacier Park crew had accomplished was definitely inspirational, but to extrapolate that to the flatland political quagmire back home still seemed ludicrous.

So did the Big Trees. I looked back home in shame at the twigs I'd seen loaded on "log" trucks. Those would not even qualify as saplings in this forest. I could hardly tilt my head back far enough to see to the tops of these trees. How magnificent this Creation! How impossible! How awful that people had ever dared cut even one of these beings down!

The scents of the Big Tree forest were different from those in Yosemite Valley, but also pleasant and richer than those of a pine forest, sweet instead of sour. I looked up for birds but saw none in the distant canopy. On the ground I saw a strange kind of blue jay and some little birds with what looked like executioners' hoods. I asked Betty about those.

She said, "Juncoes, aren't they cute?"

Back in the museum I looked at some of the exhibits while Perry and Betty had a quiet conversation. When they finished, Perry and I went outside to hitch a ride back to Wawona. "No kilo for Betty?" I asked.

Perry looked at me like "Another cop question," but answered, "She doesn't need it, some people get to the place they need to be without herbal help; she's one of those people."

"I'm glad you introduced me to her, she does seem to be a special person. And, you know, if I ever decide to go back to college, maybe I'll study ecology. I like what I feel around Betty and Rick. Both have some kind of special..."

"Aura," finished Perry.

A Park Service patrol car came up. The Ranger said, "Hello, Perry, you and your friend hop in." I felt uncomfortable again. I did not know if Perry might have more marijuana in his backpack or exactly what the Ranger might know or suspect.

"Hello, Stan. Thanks!" said Perry and got into the front seat. I got into the back, timidly.

"Stan, this is Mike. He's from Louisiana. Mike, this is Stan. He's the regional supervisor."

Oh, my, I thought. Top cop and here I am with the top drug distributor. I could get ulcers.

"Glad to meet you, sir."

"Yeah, he's from Louisiana, all right. Good southern manners," said Stan.

"Going all the way to Wawona?" asked Perry.

"Yes, how was the trip?" Stan asked.

"Got to see Janis and Big Brother at the Avalon," Perry gloated.

Stan turned back to me and said, "He likes to make me jealous. I just get to hear the records, and I have to be discreet about that. You are lucky to have full freedom."

Perry said, "Don't let him kid you, Mike, Stan loves being the starched-up Ranger, like all his buddies. It's a role they relish and I'm glad they do, because if they weren't the way they are, we would have..."

"Park Police. That's what you'd have and that's what's coming because things are getting too obvious, too much out in the open. The Superintendent is under a lot of pressure from Washington. It's not going to take many more complaints from Mr. or Mrs. Middle America about flower children openly smoking dope in front of their kids, and the decision will be made," Stan warned.

"You really think it's on the verge, already?" asked Perry.

"Yeah, in fact, the decision might have already been made. It wouldn't surprise me if they are hiring and training right now, just haven't told us yet. Washington's getting paranoid, not just about hippies, but some of those anti-war rallies are getting to be good-sized, especially in Berkeley. And they see y'all there along with the other guys spouting off the hatred and vilifying 'the pigs...' You can hardly blame a bureaucrat in the East for thinking he's got an evil, Communist conspiracy on his hands and trying to nip it in the bud. That could be bad for all of us. What the word 'revolutionary' means to you, Perry, it does not mean to SDS, Black Panthers, or politicians." Stan came across as being genuinely concerned, but I still couldn't figure out why a law enforcement officer seemed to be siding with lawbreakers and against the government's official policies.

As if he had read my mind, Stan continued, "All these years, this uniform has meant happy faces, smiles from every tourist family who sees it, gratitude from everybody stalled with vapor lock on a mountain slope, hearty handshakes from old-timers who've come for what they know will be their last trip up here. And now, they want us to be cops like in a city, 'bust 'em, round 'em up, teach 'em a lesson, don't turn over the parks to a bunch of long-hairs, dope fiends, anarchists...' The minute we start coming down hard, the same thing that's happening in Berkeley will happen here, an equal and opposite mean-spirited reaction, just us against them and those against these, and there goes all the decades of good will, there goes the Smokey the Bear image, all at once."

Perry interjected, "Mike, what the Rangers and Naturalists have done is buy some time. They've made recommendations that law enforcement at a felony level be handled by a new group, the Park Police, who would wear more cop-like uniforms. That would leave the Rangers in charge of handling most things in their usual discretionary manner and preserve the good feelings that exist between the Rangers and the public."

I could see Stan's dilemma. I said, "Yes, I see. It would be a shame for people to become wary of the Rangers and Naturalists, a real shame." I was reminded of a couple of police friends I had back home, wise old men who knew when to give someone a lecture and a pass instead of cuffing them. And, I was reminded of the type that didn't know, or maybe didn't care, or in one case, Dunn, the schoolyard bully grown up, who just liked to bust the meek kids like Alain.

Stan dropped us off at Perry's. I asked, "Perry, does he know about…"

"The weed caravan? No, he hasn't asked, and we haven't said anything to him. He's straight. I do think he's figured it out, but, you heard him, he's not going to bust anybody. He knows that we are not a threat to anything except the same things he doesn't like about today's America. I'd say most of the Rangers are in the same boat; they know more than they want to know about what we're doing, and they know that the less they know, the better for all of us when the Park Police get here."

"Sounds like they are going to be caught in a big squeeze play. I'd hate to be in their shoes. I can just see the police turning on the Rangers and accusing them of covering things up. That could be very bad."

"Yes, but we do have contingency plans. We think we can minimize the impact on everyone if something starts to happen."

I decided not to ask another cop question.

There was a little bit of daylight left. Perry rolled a joint and put on a record by a group called Pink Floyd. There were speakers out on the rear deck overlooking the creek. Soon some ground squirrels came out of hiding and began watching me watch them. We finished the joint and Perry said "Just stay as still and quiet as you can. I'm going to get us a snack."

By the time he got back, a deer was standing on the other side of the creek twitching its ears in time with Pink Floyd. Then came another deer and some birds. Then there were some little furry things that never quite poked their heads out of the bushes but would look around the leaves. Soon it seemed like all the animals in the forest were gathered around listening and watching.

Perry whispered, "Do you see them?"

"Yes, it's wonderful."

"They do this only for Pink Floyd. I haven't figured it out yet. It's phenomenal."

When he went to turn over the record most of the animals left, or at least melted back into the woods. "It's almost dark. Most of them leave at dark. I'm not sure why, maybe it's the Phantom," he said quietly.

"What Phantom? " I asked.

"The Wawona Phantom. Nobody's ever seen it, just heard the footsteps walking all around in the dark. You can shine a light right toward the sound, and there will be nothing there. Some people think it's a ghost. I really don't know what it is, but it lives here in Wawona for sure, has all my life anyway."

"You've heard it yourself?" I was beginning to think I was getting conned.

"Oh, yes, several times a year. Freaks out some people but we all just take it for granted."

I decided not to play into the con, if that's what it was. "Good brownies," I said.

We went inside and listened to more unusual music. I fell asleep on the couch.

Chapter 5

The Haight-Ashbury

Within a few days Perry had me well-programmed and even enthusiastic about helping with the Plan. I called home for reinforcements. A couple of friends of mine were wrapping up med school and trying to decide where to do their internships. I told them that they should try for San Francisco. I told some of the kids who were leaving high school and thinking of enlisting or waiting to be drafted that they should come on out and party for awhile. I knew a couple of swamp rock and rollers so I called them and said they should come out and hear some of this new stuff people were doing. I reassured my family that I was alive and well and not being corrupted by "those longhairs."

The Turtle had survived fine without me. I took it for a ride around Yosemite Valley. We stopped at Degnan's Store. I saw Ranger Rick not in uniform and another guy standing outside the door cornered by some teenagers. I figured the kids were talking about ecology.

"Aw, come on, just one six pack. Ain't no Ranger Ricks around here, please?"

So, the kids were trying to get somebody to buy them some alcohol and, of all people, they'd picked the real Ranger Rick. What would he do? I stopped to watch. He saw me smiling, and he knew that I was onto the situation.

"Well, boys, you know we could get into a lot of trouble if we got caught helping you out," observed Ranger Rick.

"No, you won't, who's to know?" snickered the bolder boy.

Rick and the other man cracked up. They couldn't contain themselves any longer.

"What's so funny?" one of the kids asked angrily.

Rick looked at the other man, and they both pulled their badges out of their pockets and held them toward the kids' faces.

"Oh, man. Oh, no. Really, Mister, we didn't mean it, please don't bust us, please..."

Rick and the other naturalist managed to fake some very stern looks. Rick's friend said, "Well, you know that there are reasons for the law. This can be a dangerous place for people who are not used to alcohol. We just do not want to see any of you young people getting hurt. That's all we care about. Now just forget about the beer and go have some fun, safe fun, plenty of that to be had here in Yosemite; you don't need to be drinking to have fun here, do you?"

"Oh, no, sir, no sir."

Rick said, "Okay, run along, we'll forget the whole thing." The kids ran along, still shaking.

I walked closer and said to Rick, "I heard your talk the other night. It's good to see that your wisdom extends beyond ecology. You may have changed those kids' lives, for the better, of course."

"Well, we hope so," Rick said. "Some would say we should have come down hard on them, hauled them into headquarters, made an example of them."

"I think they would have become bitter and more likely to hate authority than to consider giving it respect," I replied.

"That's what we think, too," Rick's friend agreed.

Inside the store I found the prices to be very high. I made some comment about it. The salesgirl said shyly but defensively, "We have to haul everything up here. That adds to the price."

Outside as I was getting back into the Turtle, Rick and his friend came out with their purchases and over to my car. Apparently having overheard my comment about the high prices Rick's friend suggested: "You could file a complaint about the prices. We can't do it, but if regular citizens complain enough, the monopolies in the parks will get attention from Congress. Did you know that families end up stranded here because their gas cards aren't honored by the monopoly? You either have to have cash or their brand of card."

"So, how do those families get enough gas to get home?" I asked.

"They either have to spend their cash, or if they are too low on cash, some good Samaritan will lend them the money for a tank of gas," said Rick.

His buddy clarified, "Good Samaritan Rick he means. One of these days someone's not going to mail it back to him."

"Hasn't happened yet, old man, not once. They have all kept their word and repaid me," Rick said.

I was developing more and more admiration for the people of California. They were sophisticated but did follow the Golden Rule treating each other the way they'd like to be treated.

The Turtle and I lumbered back into the campground. Bob, Sara, and Perry were all there, excited about something. "Guess what, Mike! Remember that song you liked, the Alice in Wonderland song, well, guess what, the Great Society is getting extrapolated! This weekend some of their songs are going to fly for the first time as the Jefferson Airplane! You wanta come plane riding with us?"

"I'm not too good at heights," I said seriously which seemed to be incredibly funny to all of them.

They must be stoned, I thought, very stoned.

Bob said, "We all get issued parachutes, just in case." That did not reassure me. Jolie Blonde giggled: "He's just teasing you, it's not a real airplane, that's just the new name. It's going to be in the Fillmore, like the Avalon, just bigger."

"Oh," I said, "Yes, I'd very much like to go."

"Let's take the Turtle, the Sopwith Turtle!" Jolie Blonde volunteered to my chagrin.

"Yes, we can get Roger to paint it, a paisley turtle on the side, its name, the Sopwith Turtle, in bright yellow to go with the dark green, it'll be spectacular!"

I knew it was going to happen no matter what I might say, they had their momentum up and it was a grand and happy momentum. I went over to the Turtle and asked "Are you ready for a new adventure old pal? We are going to see some steep hills. It'll be okay."

The Turtle didn't flinch even though it had probably been years since he was completely full of people. "So, who is this Roger that's going to do something to my car, artistic, I hope?"

"Oh, Roger is a real artist, you don't have to worry about that. He lives in the Haight-Ashbury. He does lots of those psychedelic posters for the concerts. You've seen them, I'm sure."

"Yes, some of them I can read and some I can't."

"We'll tell him to make sure that you can read 'Sopwith Turtle,' It's going to be perfect!"

We arrived at Roger's place in the Haight-Ashbury. It was across the street from a kind of coffee shop named The Drogstore. I thought it was a misspelling but Perry said it used to be The Drugstore but since it was not really a pharmacy people objected. Yes, like Stan was saying, a little too obvious.

The neighborhood looked a lot like the one where Perry's apartment was, but the buildings were not as tall. Some of them had brightly painted trim and many of them had colorful woven rhomboid ornaments hanging in the windows. "God's Eyes" Sara explained when she noticed me looking at them. "The Native Americans taught us how to make them."

Roger met us at the door, then spotted the Turtle. "That's it!" he exclaimed. "You were right! It is, it is the Sopwith Turtle!" and he immediately began crouching and eyeing and measuring with his hands. "How would you like it?" he asked me.

"I don't know," I said. "I'm not an artist. Simple, though, simple enough for people like me to be able to get it, whatever you are going to do."

"I understand," he said with assurance. "Let the words and the Turtle get themselves across together, as a unit, and she's right, just plain bright yellow words in a paisley pattern, here from this part of the front fender back halfway along the front door. That won't be too big or too obscure, just right, just right."

I hoped so, whatever he was talking about, poor Turtle; I hoped it would forgive me. I felt like I was making the same kind of mistake I had made when I had my bulldog puppy Padlock neutered. Twelve years and he never got over it, always had that sad look: "Mike, why did you deprive me of my reason for being?" I almost changed my mind about the art project then told myself I was being actually plain silly, the car is not alive like Padlock, it's just a machine. Roger went inside to get his art stuff. Bob and Perry said they had some business to take care of and walked down the street.

Sara grabbed my hand and drew me on with her, "Mike, let me take you to the Free Store and introduce you to Peter. He's a champ."

I left the Turtle with Jolie Blonde and Roger, reluctantly in part, but also, I really did not want to watch the operation. We walked a few blocks uphill passing little shops with all sorts of hippie things and past windows from which came sounds Sara called "psychedelic." We then turned onto a different street and walked a couple of more blocks.

"Here we are." We went inside. There were tables of old clothes and racks of more old clothes. There were shelves with shoes and boots and belts and caps and pots and pans and dishes... There was a man dressed in sackcloth like a monk, or more exactly, clothed in the spirit of one of the real Apostles. I felt it before she even said, "Mike, I want you to meet Peter, Peter, this is Mike."

He looked at me with two unspoken questions that I could hear in my mind: "How much do you know and how much should I trust you?" Those were perfectly fair questions.

I replied, "Peter, I am glad to meet you. I thank you for what you are doing here. Sara says that you give these things away to anyone who needs them. That is the kind of example Jesus set. I think the world has almost forgotten His Golden Rule. I'm glad it's here."

Peter's eyes softened but only slightly. He nodded and went over to talk to a young couple that had just walked in looking very bedraggled. Sara said "He usually doesn't say much, in words, but what he and the Diggers are doing are making everything possible."

"What are the Diggers?" I asked.

"Well, in the old days up in the mountains, they were a tribe of Native Americans, hunters and gatherers, mostly gatherers. They were peaceful and helped the other Native Americans and then the '49ers during the Gold Rush. The real Diggers are extinct now, but the new Diggers are people who gather food and supplies, these clothes and anything they can scrounge from anybody or anywhere they can get it, and then they give it to people who need it, free, no questions asked."

"That's very noble," I said. I thought, this wouldn't work back home, the bargain store guys would cause trouble, say they were being put out of business by anti-capitalists, get the scalawags to shut these people down, sad, too bad.

Sara and I ran into Bob and Perry back on Haight Street. We walked back to Roger's. He had finished one side of the car. From a distance I saw what looked like a bright yellow turtle painted on The Turtle's side. As I got closer the yellow turtle became letters saying "Sopwith Turtle." Yes, I could read it. "Neat!" I said. "Oh--Wow!" Sara shmoozed.

"You've done it again, Roger!" Bob bubbled.

I whispered to Perry, "How much does this guy charge?" I'd pretty much forgotten about pecuniary things hanging around with these folks. I had some money stashed, but not a whole lot. I could just see it all going for two psychedelic turtle signs.

Perry laughed. "Roger, he wants to know how much you charge?"

Roger feigned insult, "Me, an artiste? Charge for a masterpiece that will travel high into the outside world? No, mon ami, it is my honor and extreme privilege to have had this metal canvas upon which to work. Just promise me to take care of our Turtles, good care!"

"That I promise, Roger, they are beautiful." Roger didn't quite have the Cajun accent down, but he did have the spirit. And I had turtles upon turtle and from then on I had to get used to people pointing gleefully like children and saying "Yes, it's the Sopwith Turtle, there it is!"

We went into The Drogstore to have coffee and let the paint dry. People were openly smoking joints and as Perry observed, "making Plans." I could see on his face a great sense of satisfaction. I wanted to ask him how it felt to be a leader and to see all those people picking up on the Plan without even knowing that they were sitting in the same room with its architect. I decided that was another question I need not ask.

Bob and Sara caught a ride over to Marin County. Jolie Blonde stayed with Roger. Perry and I took the Turtle over to Perry's place. We had all agreed to meet that night at the Fillmore for the plane ride. Perry suggested that we leave the Turtle at his place and catch the trolleys to the concert. That way we could be as stoned as possible and he would not have to learn how well I could drive up and down those foggy and slippery hills under the influence. Wise, very wise, I thought and admitted that to him. I appreciated heavy head shepherding.

The last trolley, actually a green streetcar, newer than the ones in New Orleans but still very old, was packed with kids smoking joints all headed for the concert. I felt like I was on a high school field trip without chaperones. This is the America my friends are fighting for, dying for, this freedom, I thought, and these kids don't even realize it. Perry seemed to read my mind, or maybe it was my face. "Contradictory, isn't it, this America of ours?"

I nodded and he handed a joint over to me. A stranger had passed it to him. I inhaled and then passed it to the kids in the next seat. Contradictory, yes, this America is one contradiction after another, I thought.

We all piled out of the trolley and made our way through the ticket line and into the auditorium.

It was indeed bigger than the Avalon, and more densely packed with people. I felt a greater complexity of spirits, even some not so pleasant for a change. No, just your imagination, I told myself. Some group had already played a set. Perry said we hadn't missed much, just a group from L.A., some rough rock. "L.A. groups aren't mellowed out yet, they'll get it eventually," he said unconvincingly. Maybe that's what I was feeling, sort of a residue of non-mellowness from L.A. Would the plane ride be mellow?

Bob and Sara found Roger and Jolie Blonde, then found Perry and me. "Let's get up front," Sara urged. We followed. A different kind of leader, Sara was, unlike Perry. Sara was right on the surface, not superficial, but all there right in front of everybody, nothing held back, nothing hidden, just gloriously innocent and kind and perfect. Not love at first sight, but another one of those things that happened to me every year or so, another kind of secret, hopeless romance, another one "out of my league."

"Have a few more tokes, it's almost time," Bob said. Right away I tasted something a little different. Perry saw my question. "Hash. We lace it with a little bit of hashish for something special like this. Hold it in." It was expanding in my lungs. I had to exhale. "Have another toke, a little less volume, give it room to expand." Experience, these guys definitely had experience. I held it in.

On the stage people had gotten the equipment ready. When one of them began putting on his guitar and another sat down at the drums, the crowd cheered, the house lights went down, floodlights lit the stage, and more musicians came out to louder and louder cheering. A stunningly beautiful black-haired girl came out to the microphone at the front of the stage. Music, a light show overhead, and an incredible voice immediately sifted into all of us. The cheering evaporated and everyone was fixated on the girl's words taking off on the wings of the music. It was an airplane, gathering speed as it roared down the runway, lifting off, screaming like an F-105 Thunderchief, ready to deliver and drop its load of napalm... I put that thought out of my mind and replaced it with pure passivity; whatever they were doing or going to do, I would just ride along. I would close my eyes, then, afraid I would miss some of the elegant light patterns, I would open my eyes and shake my head in gratitude, knowing that I was in a special place at a special time, that it could not last...a special spirit that I wanted to last forever.

She sang and they flew. We swirled through the colored globules within globules sweeping around the ceiling. We danced between the columns of indigo and chartreuse that swung like detached pendulae back and forth from wall to wall. We heard her words and we felt his notes, and his, and his, and theirs joined. The performers were each individual yet they formed a unit, like rivets holding each other together as a wing, or jets driving each other forward through the clouds. Each song blended forward into another. During one of the transitions Perry smiled, "Not President Johnson's but our Great Society has taken flight." I thought, this is ecology, interconnectedness, taken to outer space.

Chapter 6

The Back Country

The Turtle hauled us back to the mountains. We dropped Bob, Sara, and Jolie Blonde back in Yosemite Valley and made it into Wawona about dark. Perry said it was time for me to meet Murphy and the Trail Crew, the ones back from Viet Nam. To do that, next day we would have to hike about six miles away from "civilization."

That night Perry cooked up some more brownies and put them into his small knapsack for me to carry. He loaded his large, framed backpack with other supplies and next morning tied both our sleeping bags onto it. Perry said "We're lucky, this week they happen to be working near here."

We hit the trail behind his house and followed the creek uphill until it seemed to disappear. We kept climbing and I began to notice the altitude's effect, I became slightly short winded.

"Out of shape and not enough hemoglobin, body still thinks it's at sea level I guess," I explained as I had to stop and rest.

Perry indicated that he understood. "We're about halfway there, it's going to flatten out a bit, you'll make it okay."

I was enjoying the things that I was seeing but regretting having to push onward. I wanted to just stop and take in the silence and the grandeur of it all. I needed hiking boots and time.

As we neared the crest of a ridge I heard other people--men, and it sounded like squabbling of some kind mixed with laughter.

Perry cautioned "Remember, some of these guys are overly sensitive. Just be kind, no matter what."

That sounded easy enough. Still, I could tell that he was giving me a serious warning.

Someone stepped in behind us, from behind a boulder and surprised us with a shout: "Hey, hippies! Where you think you're going?"

Perry turned around with a big grin, so I managed a smile.

Perry said, "Big Roy! How's it going? Trying to scare us to death?"

Big Roy laughed. "What you got for us? We already got the good stuff from Bernie."

Perry said, "Brownies, your favorite recipe."

"Great! Multidimensional high energy food!"

A battery-operated radio was playing some hard rock. Perry said "Sounds like Iron Butterfly. That's some of the Southern California music." I thought that it did sound more aggressive than the Bay Area music he'd been emphasizing.

We walked on to where the other members of the Trail Crew were having an axe-throwing contest. They'd stuck a piece of bubble gum about head height up on the side of a big Ponderosa Pine and were taking turns from about thirty feet away hurling their axes at the bubble gum. The accuracy was little different from throw to throw or from thrower to thrower yet they would argue about inches or fractions of inches as if there were some great significance involved. I thought nervously that I would certainly hate to cross one of these men and have them zero in on a bubble gum sized spot in the middle of my skull.

As a group they seemed not to acknowledge our arrival. One by one, however, they would come over and say hello to Perry who would introduce me to them.

"Snap, this is Mike, he's from Louisiana." "Mike, this is Snap Bean, he's from New Hampshire."

"Lou, this is Mike, he's from Louisiana." "Mike, this is Lou, short for The Lieutenant, he's from Ohio."

"Murphy, this is Mike, he's from Louisiana." "Mike, this is Murphy, the legendary Trail Boss Murphy from just about every National Park in the West, he's done 'em all. He and The Hearse."

I had to ask, "The Hearse?"

Murphy smiled but then got a sinister look. "I have an old hearse, downhill. I keep it behind the hotel at Wawona. Sometimes some of us go down and ride it just outside the park to Fish Camp. There's a little bar there that our friends Leo and Lena have. Maybe you'd like to ride with us sometimes?" and he was looking at me with a pirate's scowl.

I remembered Perry's warning to be kind: "Sure, I've never ridden in a hearse before, guess I might as well get some practice."

Murphy's scowl melted and he laughed, "He's okay, glad to meet you Mike, glad you've got a sense of humor."

Then he got serious again. "Perry, Stan sent that new man up with Zack and Jim yesterday. His name is Dudley, but he announced right away that it's pronounced 'Deadly.' Other than that he's had almost nothing to say, so far. He does hate hippies, though. Figures you all have turned America into a nation of wimps, know what I mean?"

Perry said, "Yeah, I'll talk to him. Does he smoke yet?"

Murphy said "Sure, hitting it pretty hard, says he misses the opium, wanted to know if we had any to get him back right. VA wouldn't let him have any, says it's been six months since he was right."

Perry was thinking, hard. "I could get him some but sounds like that's the wrong path for that guy. Let's just try to mellow him out the usual way."

"Okay, but be careful."

"How's Snap Bean doing?"

"It was getting close but when we got the kilo, he recalibrated."

Murphy, Perry, and I walked over to a brooding Dudley who was staring at a distant mountain peak. Murphy said, "Deadly, here are a couple of those dreaded hippies. They are actually not so bad. They want to meet you. This one's Perry and the short haired one is Mike. He's from Louisiana."

Dudley turned and looked at us. He looked at me longer and asked, "What part of Louisiana?"

"Lake Charles, near Texas."

"Yeah, I know where it is, I'm from Chireno, little place near Nacogdoches."

I replied tentatively, "I've been through Nacogdoches and the Big Thicket, still got panthers in there I hear."

"Yeah, out here they call 'em cougars or mountain lions. I haven't seen one here yet."

Murphy said, "Perry here brought us some special brownies. Want some?"

Dudley seemed to realize we were all trying to be friendly. "Sure."

We went back over to the axe-throwing contest. Big Roy handed me an axe and demanded, "Try it."

"I don't think I can throw it that far," I resisted truthfully.

"Well, move up about halfway, then."

I did that and then tried to throw it the way I'd seen them doing it. I not only did not reach the tree with my throw but flung it off to the side by several feet. I was embarrassed. I expected them to laugh, but they did not, which made my embarrassment even worse. I went and retrieved the axe.

Big Roy said "Watch closely, how I hold it, how I move it, and how I follow through, it's all part of a sequence that makes it work." He demonstrated. I tried again and at least reached the tree but the axe did not stick, it hit on its handle.

"You'll get it, just need to keep throwing, get that rhythm, get the angles, the twirl, and the release right."

Perry called them all over to the knapsack for brownies, and they left me to practice.

Dudley came over with a handful of brownies. He said, "You know these guys?"

"No," I said. "I've just met Perry about a week ago, and this is my first time in the Back Country."

"Well, that Lou, that Lieutenant, he reminds me of the last one we had, we had to frag him," Deadly said, his eyes glancing back and forth between the Lieutenant and me, as if he were watching to see how I would react. I'd heard of fragging. It was a terrible thing that some of the soldiers in Viet Nam had done when one of their own men had angered them or made them feel overly endangered. They would kill their own man with a fragmentation grenade to solve the problem. I was frightened but decided that I should immediately ask, "What's frag mean?"

"We had to blow him up before he got any more of us killed. He was so green he would not listen to us. We'd been there long enough to learn how to stay alive and he kept putting us back in the same mistakes the other lieutenants had made and kept getting more of us killed. He wouldn't listen."

"Couldn't his supervisors set him straight?"

"Weren't no supervisors there, they were safe back at base, at least when all this was happening. We were out on Recon. They were safe, doing all their thinking and planning. We were just dying."

"I'm sorry. I guess, like most Americans, I just didn't know. We still don't know."

"Yeah, I don't know either. I mean, if we are going to stop the damn Communists, it's going to take a lot more than what's going on in Nam, it's going to take some nukes in China and Russia, but does anybody over here plan to do that? I don't think so, so instead they send us to die; it's just hard to see, hard to see."

"When I get to that kind of dead end trying to figure things out I just fall back on asking the Creator to help me figure it out. Sometimes He does, sometimes He doesn't and I just have to let it go, unfigured out."

"You talking about God?"

"Yeah, Jesus."

"I used to go to church, in Chireno. Long time ago. Seems like forever," Deadly said.

"It's been a long time for me too, but in a way, this beautiful place, these mountains, these great big trees, it's sort of like church, without a roof."

"I guess so. Peaceful. But... Mike, it's good talking to you but I'm going to hike over there. I need to be alone for awhile."

Dudley walked out of sight. Perry came over. "You must have handled that well. Guess the Texas-Louisiana connection was the key."

"Yes, that seemed to get things started. He's had some really rough conflicts."

"All these men have. War is so stupid. We've got to get them to say it, though."

"Perry, I think that a soldier will have a hard time ever saying that what he was trained for and what he did and what he went through was stupid. Even if he believes that his particular war was not conducted properly or might even have been ill-advised, I don't think he will equate himself with stupidity."

"No, I did not mean that the soldiers are stupid, just the warmongers, the leaders."

"I know that's what you meant, but I'm trying to tell you that getting these men to approach criticizing the war publicly will take some finesse; it won't be practical to reduce it to its simplest terms. We will need to think this through."

"Mike, did you just hear yourself?" I had heard myself and realized that I had more than joined the planning effort, I'd become what my uncles would have called a co-conspirator.

"College was boring. This is a challenge," I said, "one of your bridges, Perry. Maybe I'll get some practice and insights that I can use on the scalawags back home." I picked up the axe again and threw it, hard, and it stuck in the tree, close to the bubble gum. I wondered if I should warn Lou. I decided that it would be a breach of confidence, that I would leave Deadly and Jesus to talk it out among themselves. Axe-throwing was a new dimension.

Chapter 7

The Avenues

Several weeks and adventures later I got word that my two doctor friends, Nathan and Alexis, had pulled it off. They were coming to do their internships in San Francisco. They wanted me to find them an apartment. Alexis let me know that some of the rock and rollers and their groupies from Lake Charles had already hustled out west in a decrepit VW bus. They'd asked her to tell me how to find them in San Francisco.

The eldest, Thaddeus, was a returned veteran of Air America's early, unofficial war in Laos and Cambodia. When he first got home he'd started something in Louisiana called skydiving. He played bass guitar. His younger brother, Donnie, was a drummer. Terry played lead guitar. Mongoose played rhythm guitar. William and Kenny played air guitars but their positions in the band were secure since the bus belonged to William. Kenny had the gas and food money. They all called themselves "The Wizards" because they featured themselves as inhabitants of a fantasy world, Oz. Within a day of having arrived in San Francisco they'd taken up residence in an abandoned building in the Mission District.

I drove the Turtle down to San Francisco to link up with them and to look for an apartment for the docs. Donnie was busy building himself a "sleeping loft" in the building. Thaddeus had somehow tapped into some nearby electricity and was making all the old outlets hot and safe. William and Kenny were too stoned to be of any use whatsoever.

Mongoose and Terry were working out something on their acoustic guitars.

"Hey, Mike! Come on in! What do you think of our new place?" asked Terry.

"Looks good. I can't believe you found a place to rent so fast. I have to find one for Nathan and Alexis. They'll be here next week."

"Rent? Hell, this place is free. Rent free, we just took it over from the rats," laughed Donnie.

William became slightly conscious. "Yeah, and roaches."

Kenny professed, "Little roaches, not like the big ones at home."

I asked "So y'all are squatting? What if someone finds out you're here?"

Mongoose said, "Depends on how it develops. Doesn't look like anyone cared about the place or even looked at it for years. Why should they start now?'

In an odd way that sounded logical. I went over to Thaddeus. "Bring your chute with you?"

"Nah, couple of guys disobeyed me, got themselves drowned, landed in the river, current pulled them right under. I'm leaving it alone for awhile. People don't listen. Natural selection. Death of the unfit."

"So, do these kids listen to you?"

"They'd better. I'll kick their asses and they know it. If they want to be serious about The Wizards, they'll do what I say. Music is about the only thing that might bring their minds into some kind of harmony with reality."

"Speaking of harmony, when I was parking my car I heard some live music coming from somewhere near here. Wanna walk around and see if we can find it? The music here is really different and some of it is unbelievable."

"Yeah, okay, just let me get this hooked up to my new ground circuit."

Thaddeus and I walked out into the street and turned in the direction of the music. It seemed to have a Latin element to it. We got closer and saw that the music was coming from an open air church bazaar. The music was definitely Hispanic but also was rock and roll and very melodious. Thaddeus said, "Definitely different, excellent stuff."

We went into the bazaar and I bought us some fajitas. On the makeshift stage was a group of young men in colorful clothing, not hippie style, more like Mexican. A few dozen people were watching and some were dancing. Other people were milling about the bazaar taking for granted the music, ignoring it, which I thought was remarkable since the sounds were so pleasant and orderly.

At the end of one song, though, the entire crowd applauded heartily. I asked a girl, "Who are these guys?"

She said, "The leader there is Carlos Santana, the one next to him is his brother..." She knew every name. "They're from down south but lately they've been playing up here a lot. I think that soon they are going to play at the Fillmore."

"I don't doubt that a bit, they are really good," I said.

"Si, muy bueno!" she agreed.

Thaddeus had gone over to talk to Carlos for a moment. "I had to tell him from one musician to another that I was very impressed. He is a real gentleman, too. I wish I could get our boys to have half the discipline these guys have. That's what it takes and these men have it. No limit, they are going to be big. Maybe if I can get us a gig somewhere soon The Wizards will get more serious."

The band played several more songs and then stopped. We walked on back.

"Thaddeus, I've got to get onto that search for an apartment for Nathan and Alexis. Tonight I'll be staying at a friend's place. His name is Perry. Here's the phone number of his apartment here in town and here's the one for his place up in Yosemite. Don't give it to anybody else but if you need me, he can get word to me within a day or two. Perry says that we are going to a concert at the Avalon tomorrow night. A group I've been wanting to hear in person is playing, Country Joe and the Fish."

I described the Avalon to Thaddeus and told him how to find it. I suggested that they take the trolley and buses rather than drive but Thaddeus said, "We made it this far in the VW, I think we can navigate a few more hills."

"Suit yourself. Do you need some weed?"

"Not yet, you got a connection out here?"

"Corn and weed, all you need."

"Great, see you tomorrow night."

I got the Turtle and went on to Perry's. He was inside with a very clean cut looking older gentleman in a police uniform.

"Mike, I want you to meet Captain Ross. Captain Ross, this is Mike, I was telling you about him."

"Hello, Captain. Glad to meet you."

"Hello, Mike. Glad to meet you, too."

Perry continued "Captain Ross is concerned about a new drug that has begun to arrive in the Bay Area.."

I wondered if it were LSD. I'd heard about that, but as nearly as I could tell, that one had been on the streets for months, maybe even a year or two.

"Yes," said Captain Ross. "It's called Speed, ever heard of it?" I hadn't.

"He wants us to keep our eyes and ears open, it has killed some kids down in L.A. and the San Joaquin Valley."

After about half an hour Captain Ross left.

"Who all DO you know and work with, Perry?"

"It pays to have a variety of contacts. Like I've told you: trust, love, truth, peace--it works."

"What did you tell him about me? Does he know I smoke dope now?"

"Sure, he knows we all smoke, nothing to worry about. He's got bigger problems, lethal ones."

I was not very reassured.

Perry changed the subject. "Did you find your friends?"

"Yes, they were at the address they'd called and told Alexis to pass on to me. Thanks for the relay. It's an abandoned building. They've taken it over. They're squatters."

"Old California tradition. Maybe they'll rejuvenate the Mission District, needs it."

"Maybe they'll get kicked out or busted for burglary."

"Nah, the cops don't care about that, rather have them strumming guitars inside a building in the Mission District than panhandling on Market Street. You need to be less cop-conscious, less paranoid."

"I told Thaddeus about the concert tomorrow night at the Avalon. He'll probably have them all there. You can meet them. We need to get them a kilo."

"Sure," Perry replied. "By the way, I have a lead on an apartment for your doctor friends, out in the Avenues. It's three flights up but has a rooftop view of the Golden Gate and you can hear the foghorns when the wind is right. Not too expensive, run by an old Russian immigrant, friend of mine."

"Sounds good," I said.

"We'll go over in the morning, you can check it out, make the deal if you want to, get that off your mind."

We did that. I was relieved to be able to call Nathan and tell him to just wire the old Russian the first and last month's rent and they could move in when they arrived; that was under control.

I waited outside the Avalon and led The Wizards inside when they arrived. Sara had told the lady in the ticket booth to give my friends "the special deal" for first-timers.

Kenny embarrassed me by saying to Sara as she took his ticket "Wow, Mike told us you were beautiful, but as screwed up as he is with girls we didn't believe it. He was right for once!"

"Thanks, Kenny, have fun!" she told him.

"Yeah, thanks, Kenny," I told him.

William laughed. "You got him, again, Kenny."

Puerile games, they never changed, Kenny and William would never grow up. Still, I could not deny that I was awkward in personal relationships, especially with women, whether they were catechism nuns or drop dead gorgeous older cousins with those lecherous smiles.

I introduced The Wizards to Bob and Perry. Perry took Thaddeus to the wall for a talk. Bob tried to talk with Mongoose and Donnie, but William and Kenny were playing roles, interrupting, being imaginary big shots. Terry was mingling with the crowd, "assessing the mass groove" as he called it.

I went back to talk with Sara as she took up tickets. I told her that I wanted her to meet my other two friends that were coming into town soon, especially Alexis. I figured that they could have woman things to talk about. Alexis was going to need somebody to help her through the culture shock since she'd been a sheltered bookworm most of her life.

She and Nathan weren't married, just "good friends" and compatible roommates although some people doubted that was the full story. Sara said she understood and would be glad to help. "It'll be good to have some doctors around, you know, just in case."

Yeah, just in case. I remembered an incident when Alexis and I came upon a traffic accident. She stayed in the car while I did the best first aid I could. "I can't help them, we don't have the Good Samaritan Law in this state yet," was her excuse. I could see that the real reason was a fear that she would do more harm than good, she was only a second-year student at the time. She'd probably jump right in now, I hoped.

Some of the band members were tuning up and on the ceiling were occasional tests of the liquid projections, just quick flashes, getting things focused and aligned in their assigned zones.

William and Kenny had found and begun annoying some young girls over by the ultraviolet paint area. Bob, Perry, and Thaddeus were smoking a joint. I joined them. Hash-laced again.

The house lights came down. The crowd began whistling and cheering. One of the Fish on stage yelled, "Play Ball!" and slung an imaginary ball toward a guitar player. The player used his guitar like a bat and whacked the ball with a snappy note. The keyboard player sent the ball up in an arc and on the ceiling a tight white spotlight zipped across to the back balcony. "Home Run!" yelled someone into a microphone and the crowd went nuts. The musicians played strikes, balls, pop flies, and more home runs. We can't all be this stoned, I thought, not all of us at once. This is too real, too bizarre. Who'd ever heard of a sonic ball game? We loved it.

William and Kenny came running through the crowd yelling, "Did you see that? Did you see that?'

Everybody was laughing and cheering. The light show on the ceiling seemed to be laughing and cheering. Again I knew that I was in a special place at a special time and that it could not last.

Sara had come in to see what was going on. She looked angelic in her innocence, her long brown hair and ankle-length dress putting me in mind of my Pentecostal cousins... how I wished they could be here too, feeling this kind, loving, blessed manifestation of the Holy Spirit.

The ball game ended. People were drained but happy. Country Joe and the Fish played more songs, including the one I'd heard in Yosemite, but I still could not figure out Martha Lorraine.

Thaddeus gave me a look of "Special time, can't last, got to try, though, got to try to take this home..." and we passed the same thoughts back and forth to Terry, Mongoose, and Donnie. William and Kenny were headed back for the UV girls.

As we left the Avalon, Perry transferred a kilo to Thaddeus at the van. We agreed to head up to Yosemite in a few days, after I'd gotten Nathan and Alexis situated.

I met them at the airport. Nathan saw the turtle on the Turtle. "Sopwith Turtle! Don't tell me you've gone full-blown hippie!"

"Something like that, just having fun!"

Alexis said, "Might as well. You deserve it. You always take things too seriously."

I pointed out City things to them as we drove out to the Avenues. "The Geary bus will get you to the hospital easily, should take only four or five minutes. Once you get the hang of it, the mass transit system here will take you anywhere you need to go. Better off not having your old car out here. If you have to go outside the City, the Turtle is at your disposal."

We got to their apartment and hauled their luggage up the three flights of stairs. It was a very old building, built not long after the Great Earthquake. Against my better judgment I decided to mention that. "They learned to build these tall places to flex, so don't be surprised if an earthquake happens and it sways back and forth; it won't fall down."

"Gee, thanks, I really needed to know that," said Alexis. Actually, she did; I knew that she was a very insecure person, likely to panic if she ever were in an earthquake. Her mother's place had flooded during Hurricane Betsy. She hadn't handled that realistically, but then, of course, nobody in New Orleans had handled it realistically, never would; all had an inborn instinct for denial.

Nathan said, "Let's see that rooftop view you told us about." We went up and took it in.

"Mike, you've outdone yourself. This is great, lots better than what we expected. Thank you."

"You are most welcome, Nathan, but Perry's the one who makes things like this happen. I'll introduce you so you can thank him yourself. I've got all sorts of things to show you and tell you, a little at a time. Expect to be overwhelmed, but I'll just let you get your bearings for a few days. I know that you are going to like the Bay Area and when you get your schedules, we will figure out how to get you up to Yosemite as soon as possible. It is a different kind of magnificent."

I told Alexis that I had a friend, Sara, who wanted to meet her. "Friend?" she teased with a sly smile. "Yes, just friend. She's Bob's girlfriend. Y'all are going to like them. Bob and Sara live over there, past the bridge, Marin County, another great place."

We went back downstairs. They unpacked, we rested awhile, then walked over to Geary Boulevard and had supper at a little Italian restaurant. Nathan insisted on paying.

"You won't be able to keep that up on an intern's paycheck," I chided.

"Have to celebrate. Like Alexis says, you always take things too seriously."

It was good to have some old friends back, some normalcy, a chance to "recalibrate."

Chapter 8

Fish Camp

Nathan and Alexis soon found that their schedules were going to be impossible, just as they were for interns everywhere, professional enslavement. It would be weeks before they would have two days off together. I insisted that they reserve those days for a trip to Yosemite. They promised that they would be ready to go, no excuses. I hoped so. I'd seen how med school browbeat them into submission, gave them such a sense of guilt disguised as responsibility, that they'd almost forgotten how to be themselves. At least it wasn't like what I'd seen law school do to some of our other friends, turn them into zealots for compromise, compromise for the sake of compromise, even when holding to principle would have been the moral thing to do, the thing that would have prevailed. Victory without compromise was a forsaken concept back home. I needed to get back to the mountains.

In Wawona I found Zack and Jim helping the grizzled old wagon master, Karl, at the Pioneer History Center replace some leathers in the stagecoach harness. Karl had seen, as a child, the hangings of the last stagecoach robbers. "Yes, it was this very stagecoach. Took me almost a year to get it back in shape, they'd let it sit and half rot to the ground."

Zack said, "He had to make by hand the replacement parts, some from memory, some from the old photos. He's done the same for all the wagons and carriages you see under this shed."

Jim said, "Karl was doing it all out of his own pocket until the Park Service realized how much a part of history he was saving, by himself."

"You must have seen a lot in your years up here, Karl," I said.

"Plenty, but things are changing, so fast, so fast..."

"Thank goodness you saved some of it. I'm glad they finally recognized what you were doing," and again I felt encouraged that somewhere, at least, people still got things right.

"Me too, " said Karl. "It was hard, thinking that I wouldn't be able to afford to get it finished in time, but we've made it. Now the young people will see these wagons and the old telegraph office, John Muir's desk, the old mining artifacts. Maybe some of them will think. Maybe they will help get back to some of the good things."

"It's being lost back in the South, too, the good things," I said empathetically.

After Zack and Jim wrapped up at the History Center, we went over to the hotel and had coffee. Elena was off duty but saw us and came in to tell us that Murphy was charging the battery in the hearse. He was going to take some of the hotel workers down to Fish Camp that night. "Want to ride with us, Mike?"

"Yes, I've been looking forward to seeing this hearse, and the Fish Camp."

"Be right outside here around nine tonight. See you then."

"Are y'all going too?" I asked Zack and Jim.

"Planning on it. We're going to pick up Perry and his brother Tim. Should be a trip and a half."

That evening I left the Turtle at Perry's and walked over to the hotel. Elena and a couple of her co-workers came from the dorm. We talked for a minute. Right on time an old, macabre-looking hearse solemnly cruised up to the coffee shop entrance. Murphy and Big Roy were the only ones in it, both grinning like overpaid undertakers. Some startled tourists stepped back and watched, trying to reconcile an image of mountain men, hippies, and an antique hearse.

Elena opened the rear door and sneered, "Climb in everyBODY." Her friends climbed in and moved up to the front. I climbed in and lay down like a corpse with my feet facing forward. She smiled and closed us in, then walked around, Big Roy acting the gentleman, bowing and helping her in to take her place in the center of the front seat.

Within a couple of miles the hearse was fumed with grass smoke. The gigantic joint made its way back to me. One hotel kid, Thin, said "Here, get yourself embalmed." I took a long toke, then another before handing it back to him. Up front they were discussing which 8-track tape to play. The first one was a group out of Chicago, the Paul Butterfield Blues Band. I made a mental note to be sure to go hear them if they got to San Francisco especially after hearing the song, "The Supernatural." It seemed to get right into phase with the pace of the hearse and the hairpin curves that Murphy was negotiating at just the right speed for me to be able to fully relax. Yes, I thought to myself, a hearse ride isn't so bad, not bad at all, if you're alive to enjoy it. I looked out and up from my resting place.

Behind the trees overhanging the road I could see the end of twilight. The stars began to brighten. Elena put on a different tape. "Come on baby, light my fire... light my fire..." I'd never heard it. How could a tape be synchronized with the stars moving behind the trees, with the clouds and the mountainside? How could musicians know in advance of this ride and the turns and slopes downward and up? The joint came back every now and then, also synchronized at just the right time. Even the bumps in the road were right on time. Did Murphy know this road so well that he could time such things? The melody and the rhythm..."we couldn't get much higher..." Amen.

A few years later, it seemed, wonderful light years, we reached Fish Camp. I did not want to get out of the hearse.

"Come on, Lazarus," Murphy spoke authoritatively. "Come out of there." I seemed to remember those words from somewhere, must have been one of my grandmother's Bible stories.

The Fish Camp tavern was secluded. I was glad of that. I was so stoned I dreaded having to go inside, anywhere, and meet people, any people. I just wanted to enjoy the air, the trees, the stars. Elena took me by the hand and led me up the steps. She recognized that I was "tripped out." "We'll go in, I'll sit you at a booth and bring you a drink. What do you drink?"

I told her, "Maybe a vodka Collins. Thanks." I had the presence of mind to hand her a twenty-dollar bill from my pocket. "Will that be enough?"

"Enough for all of us, thanks, Mike."

The bar was dimly lit, something else for which I was grateful. Murphy sat with me for a minute. "After awhile, I'll bring over Leo and Lena. You'll like them. They'll like you. "

"Murphy," I asked, "I've never been this stoned... it seems different..." His head turned into a circus wagon calliope. His words became scratchy steam-driven notes, up, down, sideways... I knew that it was a hallucination and wondered if every joint produced a different kind of trip.

"Hey Buddy, you still here?" Murphy asked, knowing that I was drifting away mentally and getting frightened. "It's okay, you'll get used to it, we put a little acid in the weed. Be back in a few minutes." He went to get somebody.

LSD. Perry's words about trust came into my mind and I thought that part of trust is letting people know in advance before doing something like this to them. Elena came back with a drink and sat with me. She saw the worry on my face. "Mike, just enjoy it, it's not going to be anything drastic, just sort of a modification of sights and sounds." And of thoughts I thought, a distortion of thoughts, so I'd best stop thinking. I took a swig. The Collins mix was so sour that I felt my ears twisting off, and the vodka burned like whiskey. No good, not good to mix drinks with LSD. I was still learning, still conscious at least.

Elena asked gently, "What would you like to hear? Leo's got all kinds of good stuff on the jukebox." I could not reply. She suggested, "How about some more from that new group the Doors, did you like 'Light My Fire?'"

I nodded yes and she went to the jukebox and played that. It seemed to help me return to the comfort of the hearse. I closed my eyes and brought back the sights of the stars. Everyone left me alone for awhile and I was glad. Was I in a womb or a coffin? I kept coming back to the stars, little fires in the heavens, whose fires?

Eventually Big Roy came over. "How you doing, man?"

"I'm okay, now. Took awhile to adjust to this new stuff. Sort of caught me off guard."

"I know what you mean. Fewer surprises in life, the better. Gotta learn to handle it all, though, no matter what," Big Roy instructed, knowing that he was at that moment my acting grandfather. Some people are better shepherds than others. I needed them.

Zack, Jim, and Perry arrived. The laughter picked up. The bartender asked Zack when the next meeting of the Sexual Freedom League was going to happen. "How about right now?" Zack replied. Lena, the bartender's wife made a big show of starting to unbutton her blouse but stopped and said, "Elena first!'

Elena laughed and pointed back at Lena, saying, "I'm not falling for that again!"

I guessed what had happened. Murphy oozed, "But sweetie, it was so ..."

"They were so ..." interrupted Big Roy.

"This is not Mardi Gras!" growled Elena. "This is merely Fish Camp, California."

They all continued laughing. I was feeling better, more secure.

Someone put on an Electric Flag song, which somehow did not seem to fit with the stuff I'd smoked. Then, "Don't you want somebody to love?" came a little closer to my metabolic state.. "Sounds like that group we saw, Jefferson Airplane," I told Perry.

"That's right, good ear," he replied. Let me see if Leo's got any Quicksilver on the box. He came back. "No luck. I'm not sure they even have a record out yet. It's another Bay Area group, we'll have to go see them next time you're down there." He'd put some quarters in and lined up several mellow songs instead of the harsh Los Angeles things that had, until then, predominated the evening inside the Fish Camp. I asked about one of the songs, "Eight Days a Week."

"Beatles, early Beatles" Perry said.

"Nice song," I said. "Good structure for stabilizing the mind," I didn't say.

Murphy was shouting something across the room to Big Roy, something about recognizing that Beatles song as one of only five songs that the Many Glacier hotel workers' three-piece band knew how to play, a couple of years back when they were in Montana.

I went into the restroom, noticed that it was hypersanitized, which was not what I had expected. Probably Lena's influence I figured. The napthalene from the urinal cake was almost overwhelming. As I peed, some of the yellow drops splashed up and spun like little golden planets on the ceiling of the Avalon Ballroom, so beautiful I was disappointed when I ran out.

I remembered to wash my hands. The liquid curled around my fingers in ropelike twists. I was suddenly shocked by the sight of... myself in the mirror. I think my heart actually stopped for an instant. Yes, it was I, yet it was ... different... I looked at the pores, the cells, I looked away and went back into the bar.

Elena handed me half a ham sandwich. I really was not hungry but to be polite I took a bite... She asked "What's wrong, Mike?" I wanted to spit it out since it was alive and wriggling, part of a pig alive in my mouth. I knew that could not be true but that's what it was, alive and protesting. I had to spit it out into a napkin. I put the rest of the sandwich down sheepishly.

"I can't eat this, Elena. I'm sorry."

She could see that I was serious. "Okay, Mike. Are you all right?"

"Just new experiences I guess. I'll be okay. What's that song playing now?" I was trying hard to regain control of my mind. The various light sources in the bar were intense and unstable, changing in ways that I knew were only within my head. There was an elegance to what I was seeing and hearing, but there was also a corresponding major deficit in symmetry and in stability. That was disturbing to me.

"I don't know the name of the song, but it's by a group called Steppenwolf. I think they are from Southern California or maybe New York, who knows."

"Got to get you back on your feet again" the powerful voice was preaching in the song, sounding like he was the man ordered by the Romans to help Jesus finish carrying His cross to Calvary when the load became too much, when the human fatigue crashed through the divinity. "Yeah," I thought, "get back up, handle it, like the Big Centurion Roy had said, 'Handle it.'"

On the way back to Wawona, I took my place again in the hearse, corpse-like in body, agitated in spirit, confused in mind, but aware of extra dimensions. I need to be more careful, I thought, but this is a far more educational experience than all the school I've ever had. As we rounded a curve with a mountainside to our right, a giant silver suppository squeezed past us in the other lane. It was an Airstream trailer. It took me a few moments to fight my way out of the rectal tunnel and back to within the bouldered walls and curtains of tree branches. I focused back on the real stars as Murphy put the hearse back on its rails. Elena put in a tape of the Zombies which got me back into sync. I began to enjoy the ride home as I'd enjoyed the ride down to Fish Camp. Home, I thought, where is home now? I focused back on the stars and left that question to them.

Chapter 9

Slums

Thaddeus had "persuaded" William and Kenny to make themselves useful by getting a job with the VW bus. Somehow they'd gone to work for a Bay Area slumlord from Australia, Clive Burnheart.

"That can't be a real name," I argued.

William said, "Well, that's what it sounded like to me." "Me too" added Kenny scratching scabs off his eczema.

"I thought this cool air would help your allergies, Kenny."

"No such luck. And all that Lysol and bleach and spackle makes it worse."

"What's spackle?" I asked.

William explained: "We have to clean apartments. The Health Department gives Clive tickets. Then he sends us to haul out the piles of garbage, mop away the crap and vomit, disinfect, paint, and get the place past the next inspection, so he can rent it again. Spackle is something like plaster. We use it to patch the bullet holes or places junkies ran through with their fists."

"You're kidding," I said.

Kenny said, "No, we're telling you the truth. Thaddeus told us we have to stick with it, but it's gross, and I'll be glad when we get our promotions."

"If we get our promotions," said William, "I'm beginning to think that's just more of Clive's bullshit. He tells everybody just what they want to hear, probably even us. I'm still waiting for those gloves he promised us. Makes me appreciate the tetanus and typhoid shots we used to have to get at home."

I thought: maybe there is hope for these guys to grow up after all. I can't wait to ask Thaddeus how he got this to happen. "What kind of promotions are you talking about?"

"Clive claims that he also manages maintenance at some high-class places. If we do these jobs right he might let us do some of those. One of them is for the Jefferson Airplane. He says they've got a beautiful place, huge, in good shape, we would just have to clean out the basement, maybe next week. We might even get to meet them."

"That would be a promotion. I hope it comes through for you." I started to leave.

"Oh, Mike, did you hear, Alain is in town."

"Really, where? Have you seen him?" I asked.

"No, not yet, but he's supposed to come over soon. Mongoose ran into him in Golden Gate Park. He's under a different name, I can't remember it right now."

That was exciting news. I said, "Where's Mongoose?"

"I think he's with Thaddeus, downtown; I don't know what they're doing."

"Okay, thanks. Tell them I'll be back in a little while."

I went to Perry's and told him that my fugitive friend might be found. We talked about that for awhile and then about the overall Plan, how to undercut injustice and bring the country back to the ideals envisioned by its founders. I asked Perry to put the word out that I'd like to be informed before somebody else gave me a new drug surprise, call it just a quirk of being raised up in the country, old-fashioned manners, respect for people, the Golden Rule. He said he understood. I was glad.

I went back to the Mission District and found Alain at The Wizards' place. He looked terrible, run down and scared, raggedy clothes, and smelled like he hadn't had a bath in weeks. Everybody was trying to cheer him up. "Hi, Alain! Man, it's great to see you again. I was worried about you."

"Hi, Mike. My name now is Mark. Good to see you, too. I hope word doesn't get back home...they'll send Dunn out here to get me."

Mongoose said, "Quit worrying, Alain..."

"It's Mark, please..."

"Sorry, Mark. Just quit worrying, we're going to take care of you. Things are different out here."

Thaddeus said, "Yes, Mark. It's good you came into the City. First we'll get you a nice hot bath, then we'll go over to the Free Store and get you some warm clothes. We're all going over to the Diggers for beans and rice. It won't be like the red beans and rice at home, but it's good stuff, better than the crap that Donnie cooks around here."

"I take exception to that," sneered Donnie. "I cook the best gumbo in California."

"The only gumbo in California," Mongoose said with a negative tone.

Thaddeus put his hand on Mark's shoulder. "You got a rough deal, buddy, but it's going to be okay. You're going to be okay now."

Mark started crying. Donnie went over and hugged him like a baby.

I took Thaddeus aside. "Perry says just to let him know what we need for Mark. He'll come through with it."

"How about a Presidential Pardon?" asked Thaddeus.

"Hmm. Yeah, I guess that's the ultimate answer, or at least one from Governor Edgard."

"Governor Cocksure? Not a chance. You'd have to have some good blackmail on him to get him to come through with a pardon for anybody but his rich pals or girlfriends."

"Right, worth thinking about anyway."

I left and took the Turtle over to Bob's dad's place in Mill Valley. Bob had been working on an avant-garde film project. He wanted me to give an impartial, brutally honest critique of what he'd put together so far. I watched the short film but I held back on the brutality. "Bob, I had a hard time keeping up with it. I think that I'd have to be on the same kind of trip you were on when you wrote it or filmed it. The scenes and colors are surprising, but it lost me as far as the story or plot."

Bob did not seem upset. "That's good, that's what I need to hear. I'll have to edit in some extra scenes to make it flow better, but I don't want to drag it out. It needs to bounce like this to build the excitement. It's impressionistic; it isn't meant to be for everyone. Did you know that Quicksilver Messenger Service is playing Saturday night at the Avalon?"

"No, I was planning on going back to Yosemite, but I've been hearing so much about Quicksilver that I wouldn't miss it. I'll be there. I'll bring The Wizards, and maybe I can get Nathan and Alexis if they aren't at work or on call."

"Sara loves your friend Alexis; they've really hit it off. Sara is waiting for the right time to turn her on, what do you think? Should you be there?"

"Yeah, probably so, and Nathan, too, both at the same time. Let me see about their schedule. Maybe we can do it at their place, so they would be more comfortable. Maybe not, maybe in the Turtle on the way to the concert. Let me think about it."

I went back into the City, to Nathan and Alexis' apartment. Nathan was home but Alexis was at work. Nathan said that they did both have Saturday night off for a change. I told him what I had in mind. "I don't know, Mike. It's illegal, and we can't afford to get our minds messed up or addicted or arrested."

I told him that I wouldn't be suggesting something that I felt could be harmful to them but would instead be a very pleasant learning experience. "Suppose it's got something else in it, like heroin or LSD," he asked.

"Believe me, I'm very cognizant of that possibility. We'll be smoking from my own personal batch, pure grass, no additives, preservatives, nothing but natural marijuana." I fully understood his concern, especially after my recent involuntary acid trip. "Think about it, discuss it with Alexis. If y'all don't want to try it, no big deal. I know that you will enjoy the concert and light show no matter what. It'll be fun."

I'd planted a seed, but I had no idea about whether or not it would take root.

Saturday evening the Turtle and I got to Nathan and Alexis' place. I saw Bob's pickup truck parked down the block. I began climbing the stairs, and smelling grass, stronger as I got to the top. I knocked. Nathan opened the door. He was smiling. "Come in, Mike."

"You've started without me," I complained and handed Nathan a lid of my personal stash.

Alexis was passing Sara a joint. Sara said before taking a hit, "Mike, Bob's going to meet us there. It's going to be another great one!"

Sergeant Pepper was playing on the stereo. Sara passed the joint to me, I took a hit and passed it to Nathan who fumbled it but seemed eager to get his hit. Bob and Sara must be the premier missionaries for this stuff, I thought. Some people are born real estate salesmen and these are born turn-on experts.

I never imagined I'd see Alexis, dignified and repressed as she was, toking on a joint. There she was, waiting for more of it to happen, whatever more was going to happen. How in the world had Sara gotten these two reserved, responsible professionals to just say "Yes."

"... Sergeant Pepper taught the band to play..."

Apparently it had been happening for an hour or so before I got there. Alexis said, "Mike, I bought this album when you told me about it, but it never sounded like it has this afternoon. I want to thank you and I want to thank Sara. This is quite something."

Nathan agreed, "Quite something."

"I'm glad you like it. Wait till you see the lightshow. We'd better get going pretty soon. I hear that it might be sold out," I said.

Sara said, "Worrywort, we'll go in the back way, have another hit. I work there, remember."

Alexis laughed. "He is a worrywort, always has been."

Pot calling the kettle black I thought, but progress is being made here, if not history.

At the Avalon there was a line out front so we did go around to a side door. They let Sara and the rest of us in. A warm-up band was playing. They were pretty good, but I could tell that the unified stone had not yet developed. The musicians were not leaving enough space between the notes, not enough traveling room. Sonic clutter blocked the passageways. The light show had not started, but the UV painting was well underway, and the strobe necklace thing was happening. Nathan got fixated on that while Sara took Alexis to the restroom looking for some friend Sara wanted Alexis to meet.

I told Nathan I'd be nearby, just would be walking around to see if I could find Bob or Perry or The Wizards. I found Thaddeus with Mark. Mark looked much improved and was even smiling.

"Hello, Thaddeus. Hello, Mark. How's everything?"

Mark gleamed, "It's okay, it's really okay. It's good. It's okay."

Thaddeus smiled. I smiled and said, "They say this Quicksilver Messenger Service is the best live band around. I can hardly wait."

Thaddeus said, "I hear the same thing, but how can you beat bands like the Airplane or Santana or Country Joe and the Fish? I'll believe it when I hear it. By the way, we might have a gig lined up, little bar out by Daly City."

"Great, where are the other Wizards?"

"Over there somewhere. Did you bring Nathan and Alexis?"

"Yes, and you would not believe it. Sara got them turned on, without me."

"Excellent." The music was too loud for us to keep trying to have a conversation. I motioned that I was going to look for the other Wizards. I found them sitting against a wall sharing a hookah. William and Kenny each had their arms around girls that looked like they might be 15 years old at most. Something else for Thaddeus to have to deal with, soon no doubt. I squatted down and took a short toke off the hookah. Slight taste of hash. I left them to it.

Wandering around, looking at all the people in their great variety compounded by the variety of their dress and spirits I wondered whether or not the Creator really had been all-knowing when He said, "Let this all be." I wondered whether or not He might have ever surprised Himself. He surely surprised me, frequently. I remembered a chemistry class I'd had to take. Something I wished I'd learned was on the professor's Periodic Table of the Elements, something about heavy metals, rare earths, valence states. I'd heard of a band called "Rare Earth." Several groups were named after heavy metals: "Iron Butterfly," "Led Zeppelin," "Quicksilver..." Were they all chemistry majors?

The Quicksilver Messenger Service took the stage. There was a noticeable lack of cheering and whistling. People were paying attention, intently, in anticipation of some event. The musicians also seemed serious, subdued. In later years I heard it said that Quicksilver was never captured on records as were the other groups. I believe that to be true. They began to play.

As the minutes passed I became less and less tied to the people around me. The music seemed to be everywhere yet left great spaces through which thoughts and colors could glide. Into one of those spaces came a wraithgirl, a moonlit moth drifting then darting from star to star. She saw none of us as she floated on the harmony and stepped from the melody down to the lowest bass notes then hopped from one rhythmic stepping stone to another. Her long white robe with its perfectly-lengthed trailing train swirled silently in the wind of sound. It was beyond love at first sight. It was as if immeasurable gravity had begun pulling me toward her. I reached for her. I reached feeling an intense joy but suddenly someone grabbed me whispering a yell into my ear "gravity – grave – gravity – grave - !" I struggled to get loose and turned to see who was holding me back. There was no one. I spun back around and my wraithgirl was gone.

I cried dry tears as I wandered searching through the crowd and through the notes. I brushed away the curtains of colors but I never found her.

We were very privileged, those of us who were there that night, to hear miracles of sound, to experience the unified stone. I think that even the light show projectionists became awed and lost the link they always had with the other groups. Oh, the lights were beautiful, and the synchronizations held tightly to the music, much of the time, but every now and then the music would leave this world, and take us all with it, and who could concentrate on anything like making pools of colored oil follow? I knew that Nathan and Alexis would never be the same. None of us would be.

As we left that night, very few people were saying anything. We all knew that we'd been in a special place, at a special time, and that it could not have lasted, even as long as it had. We took another hit of fresh air. We wished everyone else in the world could breathe that air from a special dimension. It was a fragile interconnectedness, that link between wherever we were that night, and to where we were bound to return. I felt as though I had been in the presence of a Holy Spirit who was giving us an advance look into a beautiful eternity. I had gotten the message but I could not convert it to words.

Chapter 10

Peyote Tom

I drove back toward Yosemite from the south, so that I could get a more complete view of the migrant worker situation in the San Joaquin Valley. I saw crop-dusting biplanes spraying fields even while the workers were still lined up across the rows. I saw workers asquat behind small bushes that offered almost no privacy. There were snappily-dressed men standing beside immaculate Cadillacs and Lincolns, laughing, while small children were struggling to tote boxes of produce to collection wagons. Elena was right to be helping organize the migrants. What a long bridge that was going to be.

The Turtle began the protracted climb up toward the park. I passed a scruffy old hitchhiker with two big burlap sacks. Old, maybe he's not much older than I am, just having a hard life, I thought. I turned around, went back and picked him up. He was very happy.

"Hop in, going to Yosemite?" I asked.

"Yes, thank you for coming back. This is quite a turtle, not bad for metal, biggest turtle I've ever seen," he said.

"Thanks. My name is Mike."

"Mine's Tom. People call me Peyote Tom."

"Dare I ask why?" I said, vaguely remembering something about a drug with that name.

"Because of what's in these bags, peyote to start with, whatever you make of it beyond that," he said mysteriously.

"What's peyote?" I asked.

"It's the Universe. It's the Universe condensed into a little button. Sort of a cactus. Then you eat it and your gastric juices peel open the door and the universe fills you from the inside until you can't hold any more."

I was reminding myself why I'd always passed up hitchhikers in the days when I knew better.

"So, it's some kind of natural drug. Is it legal?" I asked, again figuring I already knew the answer.

"Oh, yes, for some tribes. Part of our religious freedom. I consider myself grafted into those tribes."

The man did not look like a Native American, nor like a hippie, nor like anything less than an authentic time traveler from the 1849 Gold Rush.

"Does this cactus grow around here?" I asked.

"No, I go prospecting for it. I collect it in Arizona and New Mexico. These two bags took me a year. It's getting scarcer, but maybe it's just a weather cycle."

"You mean you go out in the desert and actually hunt for the cactus and pick it and save it to bring to Yosemite?"

"This is my first time to bring it to Yosemite. Last time it was Glacier Park. That was a few years ago. I shared with people there. It was beautiful, but then I had to go back home for awhile, some things I had to get straightened out. Finally I got free again and went to collect some more. I didn't mean to spend so much time at it but something kept telling me to keep on, keep on. Two bags and my knapsack is all I can travel with, so when I got two, I stopped and hit the road. Some hippies told me that Yosemite is now the place to be, so that's where I'm headed."

We passed through Coarsegold and Oakhurst. By the time we got to Fish Camp, I'd decided that we should stop for lunch. Leo and Lena recognized me. "Hi, Mike. Back already? Who's your friend?"

"This is Tom. I just picked him up down near Fresno. He wants to see Yosemite, been hitching for days in the heat of the desert. We need some tall, cool ones, just soft drinks, maybe root beers?" Tom nodded approvingly. I was reluctant to suggest any food since I remembered the ham sandwich fiasco but Tom looked hungry.

"Yes, I'll have one of those giant pickles and a piece of that pie," Tom grinned.

"Same for me," I said, figuring a pickle must have long since lost its inclination to squirm.

I let Tom tell his story to Leo. Lena was busy cleaning things but kept an ear onto the conversation. Leo asked "What do you do with the stuff, smoke it?"

"No, first you pick off all the little hairs, they're what makes you puke. Then you eat, just a couple of them if they are this size." He made a half-dollar sized ring with his thumb and index finger, "or a few more if they are smaller."

"You just chew them up? Could you cook them into a soup or tea?" we wondered.

Tom laughed. "No, I think heat would kill the strength. Besides, the taste...not good."

"What does it taste like?"

"I won't lie to you. It is about the most awful taste you would ever put into your mouth. It's just something you have to go through, like the vomiting."

"It really makes you vomit?" I asked, looking away from my pickle and pie.

"Yes, even with all the little hairs taken off, there's still enough of something that makes it hard to keep the peyote down long enough to get the full effect. It's worth it, though."

Leo said "I'll pass." Lena groaned "Me too."

We ate our pickles and pie, got root beer refills in to-go cups and sauntered back out to the Turtle.

The car had developed a musty smell inside, combination of mildewed burlap and something else, same smell that surrounded Peyote Tom, unusual. I assumed it was from the vegetable nuggets.

Manning the South Entrance gate was Park Ranger Stan. "Hello, Mike." I was surprised that he remembered me but then I figured that's his job, remember the ones that might be criminals. "Who's your pal?" Stan asked.

"I'm Tom..."

I spoke up quickly hoping I'd override the "People call me Peyote Tom" part. "Yes, Tom has never been to Yosemite, was hitching his way up here, down in that hot valley. Man I don't see how those poor Mexicans can work in that heat."

Stan said, sniffing with a puzzled look, "Yes, doesn't seem fair, Elena's always going on about that, but somebody has to do the work, put food on America's table, and, you know, it must be better than where they come from, or they wouldn't do it."

He handed me back my Golden Eagle Pass. "Be careful, have fun, enjoy the Park, Tom, I know you will, but be careful." Stan's forehead was wrinkled. He was giving me a questioning look. I felt my ears blush. Stan waved us on, and the Turtle wobbled back into paradise.

After a mile or two Tom spoke, "This is really pretty. I can't wait to get out and just spend a day on a creek somewhere. And a night. And maybe forever, this is really pretty."

"Yes, it is. The Wawona campground is right alongside a creek." Even though he couldn't have much camping gear with him I assumed that anyone who'd spent a year in the desert picking cactus buttons would likely be quite comfortable in a place with a comfort station and drinking spigots.

We made all the hairpin curves safely and rolled into Wawona. "Anything you need at the store?" I asked and pulled in anyway before he could answer. "Let's go in and have some coffee," I suggested.

Elena was serving. "Elena, meet Tom, he was hitching his way up here." "Hello, Tom, how are you doing?"

"I'm great. This is really nice up here, and cool, too."

I rambled for a few moments, "He wasn't the only one suffering from the heat, I thought the paint would blister off the Turtle. I don't see how the migrant workers don't get heat stroke. They were out in those fields like it was nothing."

"No, they do get heat stroke, and they suffer just like you and I would suffer, it's just that they have to do it, to survive," Elena corrected.

"I'm going to take Tom and his stuff down to the campground and then I'm going over to Perry's."

"It's nice of Perry and Tim to let you stay there when you are in Wawona," Elena said.

"Yes, and it gives us a chance to work on the Plans."

"Speaking of which, I'll be over this evening, we're going to be talking about something new Cesar has in the works for 'La Raza.' Need to figure out how to amplify it outside the Valley."

"Okay, I'll just listen and stay out of the way."

"No, we want your input, you always have some thoughts from a different perspective, more Middle America, we have to take them into account, for sure."

Tom spoke again, "You two are very serious. You need to let the Universe do the worrying."

Elena looked at me for a response. I hesitated. Best I could come up with was, "Tom, I know that you are right. My friend Alexis calls me a 'worrywort' but I just am who I am. I'm used to it."

Tom said, "You can be more than you know, and soon you will."

Elena looked at me again.

"He's got two big burlap bags of some kind of spiritual cactus the Indians use. That's why he's called..."

"Peyote Tom! Tell everybody I'm here and so is the Universe!"

Elena said, "Peyote, yes, I've heard about it, something like mescaline I believe. But, Tom, you can't just go around telling everybody. Some of the campers or other tourists might turn you in to the Rangers, and then they'd have to arrest you and take you to the little jail in Yosemite Valley. We would not want that to happen to you."

"No," I said. "You'll just have to play it cool. Pick and choose people to offer the cactus to once you get to know them better. No hurry, right? Plenty of time for the Universe to do its thing."

Tom reflected, "Yes, that's true, completely true, no hurry, guess this being on the road has got me into some kind of tight orbit. I'll slow down. I guess it makes sense for somebody to be serious but I still think you two worry too much. Don't worry about me, let the Universe do that."

"Fine, Tom, and it's not a very far walk from the campground to here, so if you need coffee or doughnuts, I'll tell the crew, it's on us, the company will never know," offered Elena.

"Thank you, sweet lady, I might just get back this way soon."

We went back to the Turtle and made the short trip down to the campground. There weren't too many people there for which I was glad since Tom looked so unconventional. He chose a spot at the very end of the campground, away from the comfort station but closest to the creek. We unloaded his bags and knapsack. I told him I'd come check on him next day. He looked serene and thanked me.

At Perry's he and Tim were cooking something oriental and discussing the War, which was really, in my mind, several wars. One was in Viet Nam, and one was here in America. The one over there seemed to be militarily-complex beyond any war I'd ever heard about. The one over here seemed to be socially-complex, probably even beyond the Civil War.

On the stereo was an album by Fever Tree and the music, though feverish, was beautiful, stately, tall and enduring, even though I was very unstoned.

Perry and Tim were both wise men, but I felt that they were as naïve in some ways as they were wise in other ways. I thought that it would be easy to blindside them at critical moments, something scalawag politicians would see as easily as I could see. The forces of evil would lurk patiently and save the blindsiding for the most critical moments. That was an art with the ones back home.

"Tim," I said, "would you and Perry mind if, when you are discussing these things, I take a position like one of my hometown politicians would take, just to be a horse's ass and let you know the kind of extreme ignorance you will have to overcome if we can get this stuff to a national discussion?"

"We don't mind," smiled Tim.

Perry laughed "Being a horse's ass come natural for you, Mike? I hadn't noticed!"

"Thanks for the kind words, but no, not too natural, I've just grown up surrounded by them, I think I can mimic them without a lot of trouble. One thing, though, or maybe two, don't let me get you mad, just remember it's an act, and also, if someone else comes in, like Elena, and it upsets her, stop me and let's take the time to bring down her blood pressure."

"Fine, sounds like a good deal."

So, that's how it went from then on, discussion after discussion, stoned and straight, with just two or three of us, or in a pow-wow of six or seven sitting around smoking a peace pipe. I did rankle some people who decided they didn't want to be around me, but I felt that it was important to undergird the Plan with as much of my own reality as I could. I wanted it to work. I wanted the War(s) to be over, successfully. I wanted to be able to leave the worrying to the Universe.

One night not long after I had begun playing extreme counterpoint, Elena arrived looking quite peeved. I was dismayed to hear that she'd been told by some of Chavez's other people that maybe she should consider getting a pistol for protection since some of them had been experiencing physical reprisals down near Bakersfield. Perry told her to remember Ghandi, keep it passive but push forward. I mentioned my own perpetual quandary about turning the other cheek, forgiving my enemies, but wanting to stay alive and put bullies in their place. I was no help at all to Elena on that issue.

Tim took the side of the people who had told Elena to arm herself. He said something like "We have to be realistic. If the pigs are going to club away our constitutional rights, it could come down to the same thing that Paul Revere and George Washington had to do, armed resistance. They knew we needed to keep the right to bear arms."

I looked at Perry. He was blushing and seemed flustered by his brother's odd amalgamation of left and right wing extremism. "Let's hope it doesn't come to that," Perry said.

In the morning I went to the campground. Tom's bags were there but I didn't see him. I asked one of the other campers if he'd seen the old guy. "Yes, he left awhile ago, walking upstream." I thanked him and began walking upstream. About half a mile later I heard Tom say from a distance "Hello, Mike." I couldn't see anyone. I kept walking and around a bend I found a peaceful Tom lounging on a big boulder in the middle of the creek. "Hello, Tom, did you see me from here? I could not see you, rocks and trees in the way."

"No, I didn't see you, not in the way you mean anyway. But I knew you were coming."

I looked puzzled. Tom tried to explain, "It's part of getting better in tune with everything. Things just naturally happen. Here, I've got these buttons ready for you." He held out his hand with several little cacti discs. I just looked at them.

"They won't hurt you. The Great Spirit gave us these in the very beginning, for good reason. People get all messed up, they stray away from His order and get themselves confused, they get so muddled they can no longer see things right."

I was not being convinced.

"Do you remember when you were a child, how the colors of your crayons seemed brighter than they do now?" he asked.

That was true.

"And tastes, like Popsicles, more pure?"

Yes.

"Remember as a child how clear things were, except for the confusion the grownups always seemed to put onto you?"

It was as if Tom could anticipate my thoughts before I could think them. I did not want another stressful mind bending experience, I was still getting over the uninvited LSD trip.

"This is not artificial, this is natural, it will be in harmony with your own molecules, it will not be intrusive, invasive, destructive. It will help you."

I decided to take one of the buttons, one only.

"Chew it well, swallow the juice, spit out the rest, but for now, just keep chewing."

Awful was a mild description of the taste. Even before the discomfort in my stomach made emesis inevitable, the taste itself tempted me to just purge it all.

"The longer you keep it down, the better," Tom repeated.

Finally I threw up, then got the dry heaves, awful.

"Just find a nice spot and wait," he said.

I walked more upstream and waited. After about half an hour, I walked back down to Tom and told him that nothing happened.

He said, "It takes awhile, give it time."

I went back upstream, noticing how shiny were the rocks I used as stepping stones. The cascade at my chosen spot had a crisper sound. "Yes, I guess something is happening after all." The birds' flights seemed more purposeful. A rose-colored flower drew me and a bee into its amber-powdered lobby. The bear hidden way upstream laughed silently at me. Tom sent me a thought, "Let the Universe do the worrying, Mike."

"Thank you, Tom, I think I will. Thank you."

I came to understand how Tom had been able to know that I was approaching long before he could see or hear me. Later, when I heard about the concept of quantum particles sharing information across space and time despite the reality of their separateness, I wondered whether or not the peyote somehow made it possible to tap into that mechanism for survival purposes. Knowing of changes without sensing them conventionally is a definite advantage.

Back in Louisiana, a long time after I'd been on the creek with Tom, someone asked me, "How long did that trip last, Mike?"

"Oh, seventeen years, so far," I told them. Truthfully, it's not exactly as perfectly tuned or intense, but even today, if I can find a place of peace and quiet, Nature can be Itself and I can let the Universe do the worrying. The Native Americans knew that peyote was not meant to be repeated frivolously, it was indeed meant to be part of a reverent and sacred lifetime event. I began to think very seriously about studying ecological relationships in some formal way. I wondered if Betty or some of the other Glacier Park naturalists might have been among those who had shared Tom's first bag of peyote those years earlier.

Chapter 11

Winterland

Thaddeus sent word up to Yosemite from the City. William and Kenny were picking up a day's work later in the week, removing the Roller Derby track from the Winterland Arena and replacing it with a stage for what was supposed to be some kind of mega-event. A guy named Jimi Hendrix would be playing and also, The Doors from Los Angeles. Thaddeus wanted everybody to come on down, Donnie was going to make Dungeness crab gumbo.

Zack and Jim couldn't get their days off changed, nor could Elena. Tim had something going on in Berkeley and Tom didn't want to leave the creek. Perry and I took the Turtle downhill.

At Perry's apartment we smoked a joint with Captain Ross watching and talking. He said things were getting worse, especially in L.A. and the San Joaquin Valley, with the proliferation of amphetamine. Some of his friends were considering opening a Free Clinic in the Haight-Ashbury since there had already been one death there from the stuff and several close calls. Ross was almost begging Perry to come up with some way to counter the speed problem. Part of the discussion involved the economics of greed. Perry considered the amphetamine marketers interlopers stepping onto sacred ground. Captain Ross just considered them old-fashioned criminals. Again, I was no help on the issue.

I went over to Nathan and Alexis's place. Nathan was at the hospital. Alexis was home. I asked her if she'd heard of the amphetamine problem. She had. The medical community was quite alarmed.

"What makes this any more alarming than marijuana or LSD?" I asked.

"This one seems to have no mercy; different kids have different tolerances, and there is no way to know in advance. It just blows a blood vessel, strokes them out, dead on the spot, or freaks them out and they get gunned down by the cops or Hell's Angels or whoever feels justified."

Mean stuff.

"You and Nathan have Saturday night off?"

"No, we're both working."

"Too bad, supposed to be a good concert at Winterland."

"Yeah, William and Kenny came by last night, told us about it, a hundred times. How do I get it across to them that we don't get much sleep, need our rest? They just wouldn't take the hint."

"Tell them flat out," I said.

"I don't want to hurt their feelings," Alexis said.

"I'll do it. Besides the concert did they have anything constructive to say?"

"Yeah, well, I don't know about constructive. William said they were cleaning out the basement at the Jefferson Airplane's place and one of the musicians gave him a sheepskin coat. Kenny laughed. William started laughing, too. I asked what was so funny and they changed the subject. You think it's true?"

"That they were working at the Airplane's or that someone gave them a coat? They did say something about maybe getting to work there, called it a promotion. Maybe they got the promotion," I said as I also wondered what could have been funny about someone giving a brother a warm coat the way Jesus had instructed. It was always cold in San Francisco. I figured that maybe the musician had noticed the po' boys' light jackets and felt sorry for them. Still, what could have been funny?

Alexis seemed to want to stay on the thought about the boys having actually been at the home of the Jefferson Airplane. She said, "William said they were met at the door by a truly beautiful woman, do you think that could have been Grace Slick?" I could tell that Alexis was beginning to enjoy the free atmosphere of the time and place so different from home.

"Probably was," I said.

Alexis then said that Kenny had described some beautiful song that the band was practicing upstairs the whole time he and William were cleaning out what he described more as old horse stalls than a basement. "I can't wait to hear that song when it comes out in a concert!" Alexis said.

I hated to bring her down, but I asked if there was any other news from home.

"Oh, both their mothers have sent word that they've gotten draft notices in the mail. They're supposed to go home and then go to Shreveport for a physical."

"Hmm," I said. "Well, Kenny'll never pass the physical, but William, once they talk to him, he'll probably get rejected like I did, except on mental grounds. He's way too immature to be a soldier."

"That's why they have boot camp," Alexis declared.

"You are desperate to get rid of them, aren't you?" I asked.

"No, no, I'd hate to have it on my conscience that I sent someone to die in a war."

"Isn't that what all of America is doing, all of us, sending them to die?" I pushed.

"Please, I don't want to think about it."

"Okay, tell Nathan I came by. I'll be in town until after the concert. If you need me or the Turtle call me at Perry's apartment." I went back over to Perry's.

Perry said, "Bob and Sara are going to meet us there. You and I are taking the Norton."

Oh, no, I thought, not that big old motorcycle he had in the storage room.

"Really, Perry, I'd rather take the bus, or the Turtle."

"Scared?"

"Very."

He laughed. "I've grown up with my sickle on these streets, you'll be in safe hands."

Well after dark we smoked a hash-riddled joint. Down in the storage room we dug out the Norton. Perry fiddled with things on it, checked the tank, "Still got enough to make it to Yosemite, or at least halfway." He buckled an old helmet on my head. "Here, this should make you feel better especially if we crash!" he teased. We wheeled the machine out onto the sidewalk. After a few kicks it started, way too loud. "Get on, and hold tight, around me, like this, and do NOT lean, just stay centered, let me do any leaning, you just hold on..." and off we rocketed on the slick pavement through that eternal San Francisco mist, our echo bouncing off the Victorian cliffs, surely aggravating all the grandmas.

Perry would lean the bike over on corners, scaring me to death. I did not see how the tires did not slip out from under us. We left the perpendicular streets and blind corners and got into Golden Gate Park. It was dark; I thought of the name Black Forest, somewhere in Germany I'd heard. This forest was more sparse than the one in Yosemite, but it was black except for the splashes that swerved across our headlight. The driving mist kept my eyes shut from moment to moment, but I was too anxious not to keep trying to see what we were about to hit or if we were going to careen into a chasm. The blasting of the engine beneath me and the squeezing of my guts one way then another by centrifugal force and acceleration and deceleration was exacerbating my panic. I was about to scream for Perry to "Stop! Have Mercy!" when he did.

We'd reached the edge of the park. He turned back and asked, "How'd you like that ride?"

I was breathless, but I managed "I'm walking back." He laughed.

We resumed the ride to Winterland, at a much subdued pace. I remember smoking another hash-laced joint as he stashed the cycle. We presented our tickets, which Perry had gotten in advance, before the sellout. Inside I felt like I was going to some kind of football game. The place was several times as big as the Fillmore. I could tell that the lightshow, if there were to be one, could not be as integral a part of the experience as it always had been in the uterus of the Avalon.

"Perry, this place is too big," I objected.

"In what way, Mike?" and the way that he asked, I knew that he was not expecting an answer about physical volume.

"There cannot be the intimacy that happens in the Avalon or in a private home. This place is like a stadium."

"For the barbaric hordes, screaming for Christian blood?" Perry gestured with much animation.

That took me aback. "Yeah, I guess, something like that, definitely the opposite of the mellow you always point out."

"Glad you picked up on it so fast. This is certainly a different thing. Its roots are not all with us, but we are going to have to deal with it, incorporate it, exploit it."

I could tell that he was planning as we walked around looking at the people gathering, jostling each other around. There was a different spirit at work.

"Mike, mellowness has its place; high energy has its place. For the voyage America must take we must meld the two things. We must tack the boat in such a way as to extract the energy without capsizing. We must hurry through the rough waters dispensing our cargo of love and peace upon whichever islands welcome us. We shall bypass and leave behind the islands who choose their own doom."

Man, is he stoned this time, I thought. Thank you Jesus for getting me off that motorcycle alive.

We found Bob and Sara who'd already found The Wizards. They'd plunked themselves down dead center on the floor instead of up in the more comfortable seats. "We wanna be close so we can see better," said William.

Terry and Mongoose, the Wizards' guitar players agreed, "so we can see the fingering. This guy Hendrix does some astonishing stuff."

Thaddeus said, "Too bad Alexis and Nathan had to work."

Mark seemed relaxed, not even looking over his shoulder. Donnie was meditating.

The Doors came on, and the lightshow did seem irrelevant. Although I am not a musician, I was impressed by the way that first the keyboard player would draw the others along, then the bass player, then the drummer, and all the while the singer would supplement the creations with odd poetry, some of which he seemed to be confecting spontaneously. When they shifted into "Light My Fire" the crowd drowned them out for a few seconds, then lapsed into ecstatic attention. I was very impressed; I liked the Doors, but there was something worrisome about the spirit, some kind of lack of order--not in the music, in the spirit, or maybe just in one of the spirits--I could not clearly discern whatever was bothering me. I could not bring back the stars I'd seen from the hearse the first time I'd heard "Light My Fire." There were advantages and disadvantages to the live performance event.

After the Doors came The Jimi Hendrix Experience. Between sets everyone smoked more. The auditorium, massive as it was, looked fogged. Three guys came on stage to lots of cheering. The volume of the first few notes startled me, "Why so loud?" I wondered as my ears became numbed and the patterns caught my attention. I'd heard the song before, I thought, "Isn't that the one that was playing when Murphy's head turned into a circus wagon?" It was "Foxy Lady." I felt punched back against the rear of my dimension, then slammed forward into its uttermost frontal edge, actually physically thrown from one limit to another by the sounds alone. I felt around for something to grasp with my hands. I widened my stance. Again there was the sense of synchronicity, but this time it was one driven by brute power, like the engine on the Norton. I longed for the old helmet. Had I again smoked an LSD-laced joint? It would be the last time I promised myself. Go ahead and enjoy it, might as well. Like a haircut, it'll all grow back, maybe.

The younger Wizards were thoroughly enraptured, dancing around with perfect strangers, sweating like out in the marsh on a summer night of frogging. slapping the air like it was full of gnats.

Bob, Sara, and Perry were subdued, entranced, but subdued. I understood their dilemma.

They were watching their peace, love, and mellowness Plan be overruled, stomped and squished into the mud under heavy boots. Perry's sailboat analogy was not going to hold up, not against this juggernaut.

Were these musicians, The Experience, the Doors, and the other groups from outside the Marin County/San Francisco area, linked to the methamphetamine culture like the Bay Area sound was linked to weed and acid? If not, I thought, if not there is a hazard here, from what I can tell, a hazard that this high energy music, so appealing to so many in this giant room, could fuel an artificial stimulant's popularity... I did not have enough information... I had a sense of dread about the impact on the Plan, but I could not deny the power of the music.   Captain Ross was very right to be worried.

After the concert we split up again, The Wizards in the old microbus headed back to their Mission District quarters, Bob and Sara to Marin,

Perry and I to the Norton. I did not have to ask him to drive sensibly. Perry seemed to be in a very reflective mood.

Back at the apartment we stashed the machine back in the storage room and went upstairs.

"Perry. There's no way to control that kind of high energy. They are going to bulldoze their way through everything, consequences be damned. And you saw how those kids reacted; all of America's youth are going to go for that. It's like the love affair with the muscle car, almost a national instinct."

Perry was morose. "I know," he said. "There has to be a way to guide it, though, to make the best of it. Think about it like my Norton. The driver controls its power."

"I hate to think in terms of salvage, but what do you think of just drawing back, consolidating the gains, maybe trying to make the Bay Area and Yosemite enclaves apart from what's going to happen?"

"That we MUST try to do, but we cannot do only that. Some of us have seen this coming for awhile. I'm tired. I'm going to crash," Perry said.

He went into his bedroom. I took the sofa. Too bad we couldn't have gotten the right spirit spread farther before the other spirits took over. Still, I thought, there must be a way for the best things to survive and thrive. I surprised myself with that moment of faith and hope. Instead of singing to myself a Hendrix or Doors song from the concert, I went back to some wordless minutes of the Quicksilver concert and then some wordless moments of a Country Joe and the Fish performance. I fell asleep watching the sound of a home run traveling over the whole state back home, with hypocritical politicians staring up in awe and fear, as if they were seeing and hearing the dreaded Second Coming.

Chapter 12

Hell's Angels

William and Kenny decided not to go home and face the local draft board but to instead walk into the one in Berkeley and declare their various objections to the war on grounds of being conscientious objectors. Thaddeus told them "You do that, don't come back here, you know damn well you never had any connection to the real conscientious objectors. Don't disgrace yourselves and cheapen their sincerity by playing some dumb game just to fit in with those violent freaks on the other side of the Bay." Thaddeus sounded just like our uncles back home. Unlike the uncles however, he did recognize the legitimacy of some conscientious objectors. William and Kenny spent nights in the van from then on, except on really cold nights when Nathan or Alexis were too tired or kindhearted to turn them away.

One rare weekend when both Nathan and Alexis were off-duty together, Bob and Sara finally got them to Yosemite. They were camped in the little climbers' campground at the base of El Capitan because the main hippie campground on the river nearer to the center of the valley was jammed. That evening we all piled into the Turtle and drove to see Ranger Rick's slide show at the rustic old Ahwahnee Hotel. Most of the audience were affluent, middle-aged people or retirees. Rick skipped the singing routine and gave a grand history of the park. He told of the work in Yosemite of Frederick Law Olmsted, the same man who'd laid out New York's Central Park and New Orleans' Audubon Park. He praised John Muir but seemed to get the most silent nods of affirmation when he praised the Republican President Teddy Roosevelt. Sprinkled into Rick's talk were ecological principles with emphasis on restorative efforts. He explained that the Park Service had taken flak for a recent hunt in which deer were harvested within the Park's boundaries. Because there had been a shortsighted policy in which a bounty was paid for every mountain lion killed, the natural balance between prey and predator had been upset. The deer proliferated beyond the numbers that could be supported by the available food supply. Soon some individuals became very malnourished, then parasitized, and began to suffer agonizing deaths. The only solution was to restore the natural balance and since mountain lions were unavailable, hunters were allowed to come in to prey. It worked. The herd regained its vitality, but, alas, the Park Service was still being criticized. Rick hoped that the audience would take the lessons back home to wherever they lived. "Maybe we can learn not to interfere with nature so much, then we won't have to fight so hard to restore its dynamic equilibria."

Nathan especially enjoyed Rick's talk. He and I went up afterwards. Nathan told Rick that he hoped that Rick would come duck hunting with him someday, when he was back home. Rick said he'd like that, a lot. They promised to "stay in touch." How many such promises were made in that special time and how many were remembered? How few were kept.

I dropped the four off at the El Cap campground and headed back to the central campground to look for Peyote Tom. Perry had heard that Tom was proselytizing there. As I passed Ranger Headquarters, I saw Rick bolting for the door. He looked like something bad was happening. I decided to park the Turtle. I went to the door and heard one supervisory Ranger, Andy Anderson, yelling for naturalist Betty to "stay on this radio, listen to us, and try to get the Superintendent on the phone, let him know..." and he yelled at Rick, "take these keys, they are for Number 4 out there, let's go, you come in from the south, and when I radio, you hit the siren and the horn and lights, not before..." They ran out past me and jumped into the pale green station wagons.

I decided to go inside. Betty, the naturalist from the Big Trees area was standing and trembling next to a two-way radio. "What's happening?" I asked.

"It's terrible! The Hell's Angels are throwing the hippies into the river. They're going to drown. It's freezing cold water."

Ranger Anderson came on over the radio, "Get ready, Rick, let me know when you get to..." and he named some intersection. "Betty, do you read?" "Yes, Andy, I read you." "Okay, here goes, ready Rick?" "Yes, ready." "Hit it!"

I heard what sounded like fifty sirens echoing off the cliffs. I looked out the window and saw flashing red lights bouncing off trees and cliffs and the low clouds.

"How many other rangers are out there, Betty?" I asked.

"Just them, we were shorthanded tonight, just them."

Damn, I thought, it's a total bluff. They are going to get themselves killed. I ran to the Turtle and headed for the river. As I approached, I was passed by oncoming motorcycle after motorcycle fleeing the scene. The echoes of the Harleys almost drowned out the ongoing siren echoes. The Turtle slid in some gravel by the bridge. Two remaining Hell's Angels were laughing their asses off dangling a kid by his ankles. They let him drop into the rapids below. I figured his skull had been smashed--at least he wouldn't know he was drowning. I recognized the two Hell's Angels as the ones who'd been sitting like chaperones at the back of the first Ranger Rick campfire talk I'd attended with Bob and Sara. They gave me evil grins and a wave and yelled "We'll get you next time, hippie!"

I ran down to the river. The kid was struggling against the current holding on to a boulder. How he wasn't dead I couldn't understand, one of the Creator's miracles I guess. I told him to hang on, but he let go and managed to keep his head above water. I ran alongside as he was swept downstream. He came near enough the edge that I was able to grab his outstretched hand and help him ashore. By then we'd gotten into an area where people were splaying flashlight beams about and hollering for each other. They were soaking wet and shivering. I ran on downstream a few yards and saw soaking wet Rangers Andy and Rick. Andy was performing that new kind of CPR on one old guy. It was Peyote Tom.

Rick said, "He's the only one we didn't get out in time."

Jolie Blonde was there with some other soaked kids. She shouted, "Let's pray everybody. Let's ask the Universe to help Peyote Tom. Don't you think It owes him? Let's pray."

Whether it was the CPR or the Universe Tom began to cough and try to move. Andy had him roll over and cough some more fluid out of his lungs. Tom turned back into the light and was smiling like he always did. "Wow, what a trip. That water was COLD!"

Jolie Blonde was jumping up and down saying "Thank you Universe! Thank you Universe!" Back home she would have been saying "Thank you, Holy Ghost, Thank you, Jesus!"

I prayed, "Thank you, Creator, and thank you, Rangers."

Rick looked around nervously. "It must have worked, Andy. I don't see any of them."

I said, "The last two threw a kid off the bridge and left just as I got here. You pulled it off; I can hardly believe it."

Andy ordered, "Rick, go up, shut off the sirens, and radio Betty, she's probably a basket case by now, you know how she feels about you. And tell her if she hasn't reached Superintendent Talbot, don't bother him, I'll report to him in the morning. If she has reached him, he'll be here in a few minutes anyway." By then other Rangers were pulling up in their personal cars, out of uniform.

"Wait'll the news people hear about this riot and how y'all handled it!" I exclaimed.

"No," Anderson said, "We can't have news media making a big deal, it would scare off all the families and this is their park. It would ruin a lot of kids' only chance to see this place; no, I've got to keep this as quiet as possible."

I thought of Ranger Stan's prediction that the Park Police were likely an inevitability and that this would probably put the clincher on it.

"Why were the Hell's Angels throwing y'all into the river?" I asked Tom.

"Just that time in the flow of things," he said.

"Aren't you mad at them, they almost killed you?" I asked.

"No, but that water was a COLD shock, believe me, COLD!"

Jolie Blonde had him by the arm and was walking him back to camp.

"We'll get you warmed up, in my tent, I'll warm you up, Tom," she was purring.

Tom was smiling and smiling.

I asked the other hippies why the Hell's Angels were throwing them into the river.

"We don't know. They just came roaring into the campground and started grabbing us and laughing and throwing us in the river. They smelled drunk. I think they were just having fun."

I thought of the old phrase in a song "have some fun tonight, gonna have some fun tonight" but I couldn't remember what song it came from.

One hippie girl said, "One of them kept making fun, yelling about 'here's your flower power,' or 'peace this,' or 'love this.' He was scary."

I figured that Perry's Plan would have to inaugurate a specific strategy to deal directly with the Hell's Angels. What had happened that night was, in microcosm and clearly focused, that which was happening on the bigger scale. There was corruption of the peace and love movement Perry and his friends had worked so hard to generate. If we could turn the Hell's Angels into allies instead of adversaries, we would also have found a key to sustaining the overall cause. If we could sense early the approach of evil influences...

I told Peyote Tom that I'd be in the park for a few days, send me some word via the hippies headed to Wawona if he needed anything, and I'd come back to the Valley and help him. Jolie Blonde said, "He won't need anything. The Universe takes care of us."

I could see that. Of course, it didn't hurt that the Universe had a little help from its friends, especially the Rangers.

I went back to Ranger headquarters. Rick was escorting a crumbling naturalist Betty across the street to the Ranger Lodge.

"Hi, y'all, just wanted to see if you're okay, the both of you."

Rick said, "Cold, but fine, just fine, thanks."

"Good, then listen, from one American who loves the park and loves what I see you doing, I want to say thanks, and if there is anything I can do, let me know, whether it be something for your official life or your off-duty life. Some of us would like to have a way to pay you back. "

"It's our job, don't worry about it."

"Well, thanks especially for saving that old fellow tonight. I feel somewhat responsible for him, I'm the one who picked him up when he was trying to hitch a ride up into the park."

"Yeah, Stan told us."

Betty asked, "Does he really have two burlap bags full of peyote?"

Rick said, "She's off duty, you can tell her."

I laughed. "Yes, it is true, and he really believes in it like the Indians, like a religion, not like some entertainment drug."

"Well," Betty said cautiously, "I met someone in Glacier once that was giving out peyote. I wonder if it could be the same man. His name was Tom, I believe it was Tom." She was blushing and looking downward.

"Could be, who knows, lots of strange characters in these parks," I said.

Betty said, "I think the Park Police are coming soon. They are sure to go after him. Tom should probably leave."

"Thanks for the tip, Betty. I'll see what I can do. He would probably lose his religion if he got chambered in a closed cell for very long, thanks."

So, coming soon, to a park near me, the police. It was not going to be easy to get Tom and the naïve hippies to believe that their world was being surrounded by the Gestapo. I hated to be the one to wilt the flowers.

Back in the Turtle I drove through the night toward Wawona, listening to the Fresno rock and roll station. The DJ sounded a lot like Casey, one of my high school buddies from back home. He was playing the hard stuff, from L.A. There was an undeniable appeal to the music, Canned Heat was like a hyperbolic blues group, probably would do well in Hardlegs, one of those Highway 90 dives at home. Rare Earth came on and made me feel like celebrating another day of life even though the people might have let me down.

Steppenwolf was down on the pusher but not the dealer. What people have let me down? Politicians, preachers, mostly politicians. I concentrated on the curves and slopes. The synchronicity was not there. "You aren't stoned," I told myself. Correct, but there was something else involved. I was not tuned to the sounds of L.A. like I was tuned to the ones from San Francisco. I wondered if it were because those were the ones through which I was introduced to mind expansion. If so, it would be extremely important that the peace and love turn-on missionary work would start people off with the mellow, peaceful, loving sounds instead of trying to convert them from sounds of different worlds whether any drug tool were to be involved or not. I thought back to apostolic tent revival music. Most of that was ultra-high energy. Maybe my theory was wrong, maybe high energy rock could slingshot people into a holy place... farfetched... and yet the Holy Rollers were slain in the spirit of mellowness and love.

The Fresno DJ put on "In a gadda da vida" by Iron Butterfly. It went on for miles. It was powerful. We would have to tap into the source of that power, somehow. I pulled into Perry's place. Tim was still up, working on his thesis.

"Come in, Mike. I got a call from Bernie, on the lookout tower. He said a riot of some kind broke out in the Valley. Did you come from that direction?"

"Yes, I was there." I told Tim what had happened. He seemed strangely unsurprised, mumbled something about having to talk to the Horsewhip and looked like he needed to get back to work.

"Tim, I've been meaning to ask you, what's your thesis about?'

"The Role of Music in Revolutions."

"Oh, that's good. That's one lots of people are going to need to read. I need to read it as soon as its ready."

"Not too long, Mike. I'll let you know."

I was very tired. I told Tim I was going on to the back room and go to sleep, that I appreciated their letting me crash at their places in Wawona and San Francisco. He said I was more than welcome. It was getting harder and harder for me to get to sleep each night. I was more and more agitated about losing a great chance to... change the world. The Plan had too many variables.

Chapter 13

Convergences

I awoke next morning at the brothers' place in Wawona. Tim was asleep at his desk. I walked down to the coffee shop. Elena was serving Zack and Jim pancakes.

"I'll have some, too," I told her.

Zack said, "Heard you got in on the excitement last night."

"Word travels fast for a wilderness."

Jim said, "Told you we had contingencies, topnotch coded communications network, even if it is on outdated government radios."

"Rick said you got a good look at the two Hell's Angels who didn't get bluffed out right off. Can you describe them?"

"Yes, well, you know, they all look scruffy and mean and wear those costumes..."

"Colors they call 'em, it's like a flag to them, better not let one of them hear you say 'costume'."

I continued, "One of them was short and built like a cube, but his face looked like a Cajun pirate."

"What's a Cajun pirate look like, Mike?"

"Oh, I don't know, it's just an image of Jean Lafitte I've always had, little twisted black mustache, shiny black slick hair, gold rings and necklace, just flashy."

"And the other one?"

"Tall, dirty brown hair, strong-looking, long brown beard; it was pretty dark, just my headlights to see with. Why are you asking, have the Hell's Angels been around here?"

"We get all the motorcycle gangs. Stan ran out one bunch that got too raucous, warned them about the rock snakes. Fifteen minutes later they were blowing down the road out of the park."

"What are rock snakes? I've never heard of them."

Zack, Jim, and Elena laughed. "We hadn't either. Even Ranger Rick has never heard of them, but Stan says they are very dangerous and are attracted by the smell of grease."

"Oh, bullshit, are these Rangers all bluff or what?" I asked. "Thanks for the coffee, Elena."

"You're welcome. I think last night's psychology was the best 'bluff' as you call it, best yet. Did it really happen that way, just two patrol cars against thirty motorcycles?" she asked.

"At least thirty."

"So, it was the Horsewhip and the Pike," Zack said.

"What?" I asked.

"You've perfectly described the leaders of the San Joaquin chapter of the Hell's Angels. The cubical one is called The Horsewhip, we presume because his chopped hog has a coachwhip coiled up and hanging on the handlebars, and the tall one is The Pike. We're not sure why. They come up here a lot, sometimes with the rest of the gang, sometimes just the two of them. We thought they were up to something, guess last night was it."

I asked, "Why in the world would they want to toss a bunch of harmless hippies into a freezing river?"

Elena pondered, "That's a very good question, especially since I'd heard a rumor that The Pike and The Horsewhip were on good terms with hippies, trading different drugs like grass and acid. And the Hell's Angels down south in L.A. are supposed to really be into the heavy metal rock scene."

Jim offered yet another tidbit of maybe information: "Snap Bean told me that one day the new guy on the trail crew, the one they call Deadly, said he couldn't wait to get back to a phone again and make a call to his old pals in Fresno; said they were all Hell's Angels before he enlisted."

So, I thought, if Tim knows the Horsewhip, and so does Deadly, how does this all fit together? I needed to talk with Perry. I had a feeling that he'd been holding back on some things, or, giving him the benefit of the doubt, maybe he'd been bringing me along as an ally at a pace a little more slowly than necessary. We ate our breakfast.

Elena said, "A thought just struck me. Lately some of the resident Chicanos have told me that the new arrivals got some help getting across the border down by Calexico, from a gringo motorcycle gang."

"Why would a motorcycle gang be helping wetbacks?" I asked and immediately apologized, "I'm sorry, Elena, force of old habits, I'm sorry."

"You should be, some people consider that term to be very disrespectful, but apology accepted."

The intact part of my brain suppressed an impulse from the mushed part to point out that Elena had used a term, "gringo," a term that maybe some people might not like.

Jim said, "Only reason I can think of for an alliance between Hell's Angels and Mexicans would be favor-for-favor. If the immigrants need help and the bikers need marijuana, could be a perfect match, maybe a kilo per person to get across and deep into the state."

"Sounds reasonable," Jack agreed.

I excused myself, walked back to Tim and Perry's. Perry had rolled in on the Norton.

"Man, did you drive that thing all the way from San Francisco?" I asked.

"Sure, why not?"

"Hazards, heat in the Valley, snow melt on the curves up here," I whined.

"Not hot at night. You've got just the perfect personality for a Turtle, Mike. Come on in, we need to talk."

Did we ever.

Perry began with "I hear you saw a couple of our allies at work last night."

"Allies, who do you mean?"

"The Hell's Angels."

"I wouldn't call killers allies," I said defiantly.

"They didn't kill anybody."

"Peyote Tom, almost, Ranger Anderson was doing CPR on him when I got there, it was a damn close call. And I saw them drop a kid head first off the bridge, could've hit those boulders. Yes, in my opinion those guys were killers."

"Look, we didn't know anything about what happened last night. It seems to have been some kind of spontaneous aberration. They are the Hell's Angels after all. They got a little carried away, never mind, it's all going to turn out okay."

"Okay?... Crap! What's going on?" I demanded to know.

Tim had Iron Butterfly playing on the stereo.

Perry said, "Calm down. Here's the situation. You saw it for yourself. We cannot sustain past a certain-sized nucleus the cohesiveness of a pure love and peace movement. That does not mean that we cannot sustain the momentum of the movement at one quantum level higher, just that it must incorporate additional structural members, like the framework in a bridge, or the cables."

I was trying to suppress a massive internal conflict between anger and curiosity. Curiosity said, "I can wait, hear this bullshit out." Anger bent but added, "When he's through trying to explain you can get as mad as you like and have more ammo with which to work." I kept listening.

Tim joined the explanation. "I've already called the leaders of the Hell's Angels. We've asked for a 'summit' meeting with them and some other people to get this all straightened out. Every now and then we call a bunch of key planners together. They've all agreed to meet again. It's going to be okay."

"Oh, how is it going to be okay?" I argued. "They've got every flower child in the country scared shitless instead of mellowed out, you've got every biker in the country wishing they could've been there to throw a hippie off a bridge, you've got the Park Police almost all the way to the gate... Yeah, real okay, perfectly okay... *coullions, coullions...*"

Tim translated for Perry, "' I think '*coullion*' is French for 'fool'."

"Mike, let's smoke a joint. It'll help you see the Plan better."

"Plan, I'm sick of the Plan. It was a beautiful idea but this just blew it, this forming an alliance with killers. And glossing over a stupid riot and justifying compromise of principles... You have betrayed your own Plan." I was making very clear to Perry and Jim that I had reached a limit. I was again feeling rejected and dejected, and the feelings of love were dissolving into feelings of unforgiveness.

"No, it hasn't. We haven't given up on the principles, we're just going to have to accept certain realities and change the objectives somewhat. We still intend to stop the War. We still intend to wake up the American people. We still intend to bring some sanity to Washington, D.C. We've just learned that they won't let us do all that the gentle way. We have to get tough back, like they've been to us."

Curiosity prevailed again.

"Who's 'they' and how have 'they' been tough on us?" I asked.

"Speed. It's one of the secret weapons of the government, so is Angel Dust, so is Panama Red."

Panama Red was some weird marijuana. A big batch had come into the Bay Area and some kids had actually freaked out on it. Nathan had seen a bunch of them one night in the emergency room. He said that he thought that they showed signs of some kind of memory blender or eraser, probably scopolamine.

I reflected on the possibility. "You actually think that our own government would attack its own children with chemical weapons?"

"Not think, I know," Perry declared with absolute certainty.

Yes, he might actually know, I thought... Captain Ross...

"By hitting us with Speed and Red and Angel Dust they've used our own network against us. They are turning all our good work into tragedies. It's obscene."

If that theory were true, it was indeed obscene. I remembered an incident in the Haight at an apartment where we'd stopped awhile back to pick up Jolie Blonde. A large, well-dressed black man had suddenly come in and almost insisted that we each take a toke on a "special" as he called it. I passed. After the "special" made a couple of rounds, the guy left quickly and we also left but I remembered someone saying as we left that the "stranger's special" was different. I wondered whether or not that might have been one of the chemical warfare special agent forays into the Haight.

Perry continued. "This is a war. The Angels have been very helpful to us in a lot of ways. They are mobile, they have contacts not just in California but past all the borders. They are fearless, they have no love for the entrenched political machines. Nevertheless, they recognize that only in America is there the supposed freedom to be whatever they want to be. That freedom they do love and, like the most patriotic of soldiers, that freedom they are willing to fight for, even die for. Odd as it seems, they saw some aspects of themselves in the flower children and to some extent in some limited situations became protectors, almost paternal in a way. "

I said snidely, "I guess that instinct gave way to the 'drowning the defective baby instinct', right?"

"We are going to get it all out in the open at the summit meeting. I'm sure we can keep anything else like this from happening again," said Tim.

"Trust, Mike, it's all about trust..."

"Perry, trust has to be tempered with common sense, I've been re-learning that the hard way lately, and it hurts to actually feel my trusting nature going bitter, it hurts."

I had calmed down, but Tim and Perry could tell that I'd hit a wall. I told them that I needed to go away for awhile, I wasn't mad, just needed to think about everything. I said "I don't want to give up on making a big difference either. This country needs it, and if my friends can die over on the other side of the planet for it, I know I have to do something here, just not sure what, now."

"Besides the summit, we've got another step planned. We'd like to tell you about it."

I closed my eyes. I shook my head, "No, not right now."

"It's soon. We need to tell you about it, maybe we can avoid another screwup. You can help us fine tune it, and we want you at the summit."

They sounded sincere, like maybe they had learned from a mistake. Not learned enough, yet, I thought. Let them think they are losing an ally if allies are what they value so much.

"I'll see you around. Thank you for the hospitality, truly, I am grateful. Maybe I'll check back with you in a day or two."

"That'll be cutting it close, but please do."

I drove the Turtle back toward Yosemite Valley. My mind was drifting. The beauty of the mountains couldn't hold my attention. I was worried.

A siren behind me shook me back to reality. I looked into the rear view mirror and saw the Park Service fire truck. Jim was driving and grinning like a parish jailer with a new electric cattle prod. I pulled into the next vista overlook. As I was getting out of the Turtle, Zack came over with a ticket book and faked a stern voice.

"Sir, you were driving inattentively. That is dangerous in these mountains."

"Yes, officer, I was daydreaming, but at least I'm not stoned. What's happening?"

"Got a message from Murphy. Deadly is missing, been acting weirder than usual lately. Search party forming. We're headed up that way. Where you going?"

"I just had a strange meeting with Perry and Tim." I filled them in.

"Hmm," said Zack. "I'll see if we can go to that summit. I wonder what's that other thing they've got up their sleeve. Got to hand it to those guys, always planning. Most of it works, too."

"I hope you find Deadly. I'll be down in the hippie campground with Peyote Tom or the El Capitan campground with Bob and Sara if you need to get in touch with me."

They let me off with a stern warning and a good laugh. As we reached a crest, they turned up into one of their gated fire roads and I continued on, soon headed downhill into the beauty of the valley with its waterfalls, mists, cliffs, river...

At the central campground the hippies told me that Bob and Sara had come and taken Jolie Blonde and Peyote Tom over to the other campground. I went there. Sara had "some luscious brown rice and raisins." What would these kids do if someone turned them on to jambalaya, I wondered. That's real rice.

We discussed the riot, smoked a joint, and were talking about the bad things that were happening down in the Haight, the speed and Angel Dust, the Panama Red incidents. I noticed a couple of Park Service patrol cars going unusually quickly back toward Park Headquarters. About fifteen minutes later we heard a siren approaching and an ambulance came past. I decided to be an ambulance chaser. I was having a bad feeling.

I saw the ambulance parked at the Headquarters. A couple of dozen Park Service employees were standing in the yard. I parked the Turtle and walked over. I saw Rick in the group and went over to him.

"What's happening, Rick?" I asked.

"One of those trail crew guys from Viet Nam. He's holding Superintendent Talbot hostage in his office."

"Dudley?"

"Yes, his name is Dudley. You know him?"

"I've had a couple of conversations with him. He's very troubled but deep down inside, he's goodhearted, just screwed up by the war, what he's seen, what he's had to do."

Rick said, "Wait here, Mike, maybe you can help."

Oh, no, what have I gotten myself into now? I thought as I tried to mentally kick myself.

I went back to the Turtle. "Old pal, you've got a *'coullion'* for a master. It's karma. I call someone a *'coullion'* and karma flings it back on me."

Rick returned with Ranger Anderson and pointed me out. "There he is. Mike, come on. Dudley says he'll talk to you. It's a breakthrough!"

Real damn breakthrough, he'll probably break me in half before he gets through with me.

I waved goodbye to the Turtle.

Rick turned me over to Andy Anderson.

Andy said, "You sure know some of the strangest dudes in this park, don't you?"

"I guess so, it's not intentional, the Creator just seems to stick it to me this way."

"The FBI has a trained negotiator on the way. Meanwhile they said to establish communication with the criminal any way possible and pretend to be his friend, get his confidence. Sometimes they can be talked down, depending on if it's a drug problem or not. If it's not drugs but a mental problem, best thing is get him by a window so they can snipe him."

We were halfway up some stairs. I felt faint. I stopped.

"Come on, Mike. The Superintendent's life is at stake."

Andy called out: "Dudley, we're back. I have Mike here with me."

"The name is Deadly. Mike, when the Ranger goes back down the stairs I'll come over and let you in. Tell me when he's gone and you better not be part of some trick. Do you hear me?"

"I hear you, Deadly. He's going."

Deadly unlocked the door and told me to open it slowly and come on in.

He was standing aside with a letter opener at the throat of Superintendent Talbot.

"Close and lock it back."

I did that. "Now go sit over there," he said. I did that.

He sat Talbot in another chair and then pulled one up for himself, putting himself in a position that would make it easy for him to go for either one of us with the letter opener should we make an aggressive move.

Unfortunately, I thought, for Deadly, that put him right in front of a window and outside the window about a hundred yards away was a large tree. I knew from hunting back home that it would be an easy shot for a sniper, from that tree to Deadly.

"Deadly, what brought this on?" I asked.

"Damn government. They're all screwed up..." He rambled on and on, some of it making sense to me and some of it so vague or seemingly-disconnected I couldn't follow. When that would happen I would stop and ask him to connect it, explaining that I couldn't make the connections. At first that seemed to irritate him but then he seemed to be determined to make me understand. I considered that to be very important.

I let him finish a point but stopped him before he could start another one. "Deadly, wait a minute, let me close those curtains." He wheeled around, saw the window and tree situation...

I thought I'd made a big mistake. He jumped up, very agitated, and ran to the side of the window.

"Okay, " he said. "Mike, you come close the curtains. Talbot you'd better not move."

The old Superintendent was causing no problems. In fact, he seemed to be studying the situation like we were just lab rats. He seemed far less worried than I was.

I closed the curtains. "Deadly, you know the best thing would be for us to talk this out without them thinking you might hurt the Superintendent. That's what's got all of them out there nervous."

"They wouldn't pay any attention to me, buck shufflers, one to another to the next and back. I can't stand it. And none of them get it, none of them see what's happening, here or over there, it's a blindness," he ground out from between his gnashing teeth.

I tried to be comforting saying, "Some people see it, more and more, what you were telling me up on the trail. I think all of America would agree with you if they had the same facts you have, it's just a matter of getting the facts to them."

"How ya' gonna do that when the big shots don't want the facts to come out until they've made a few extra billion dollars cushion on top of the billions they've already made?"

I agreed with Deadly, "That's the war at home. Believe me, you're not the only one who's fed up with it."

He pulled the curtain edge back slowly and looked out and down. "Man, if I'd done this in town they'd have already sent in cops and blown me away."

"Nobody wants to blow you away, Deadly. Not here, you made it through that time in your life. You made it through Nam. This is home."

Deadly started crying. "What can I do? I can't fight this, not the way I know how to fight, I can't fight it my way. "

I motioned for Talbot to stay put, not that he'd shown any sign of moving. I walked over to Deadly and put my hand on his head. "Jesus, help my friend. Help me. Help us all. We need you, Jesus, this is a mess, we need you." I took my hand off his head and went to a wall and knelt down and prayed silently.

A few minutes passed with none of us saying anything. Then Dudley spoke.

"Mike, go to the door and tell them I surrender. I won't cause any more trouble. They just need to take me back to the hospital."

"Okay, Deadly, let's let Talbot go out first, he can tell them. There's something I want to ask you, alone, it'll only take a couple of minutes."

He sent Talbot out, saying "Superintendent Talbot, I'm sorry I put you through this, I really am. But you need to know, there's gonna be lots more of us coming home like this, something has to change, you need to tell them to listen."

"I will, son. It's going to be okay." He put out his hand for a handshake. Deadly took his hand and began crying again.

"I'm so sorry, I'm sorry," Deadly wept.

Talbot left.

"Deadly, before you go, I need to know something. The other night some Hell's Angels were here and they threw some hippies into the river. Did you hear about that?"

"Yeah, I tried to stop that, but nobody would listen."

"You knew it was going to happen?" I asked.

"I told Murphy. I told the Lieutenant. I told Bernie at the lookout to radio it in to Headquarters. I guess they thought I was crazy."

"How did you know?"

"The Horsewhip and Pike had come to the trail head and sent for me. I went down and we had some beers. They said some dude wanted them to do it, was willing to pay them in acid, several thousand dollars worth. They smelled a rat, wanted to know if I thought it was a setup. I told them it made no sense unless somebody wanted an excuse to bring in those Park Police. I thought they were going to call it off."

He started crying again and said, "I guess I just gave them their wish, dammit; Park Police, if they needed an excuse I sure gave it to them, didn't I?"

I put my arm around him, "Buddy, the Park Police were at the gate long before you got here. I think that all that's held them back are the Rangers and Naturalists. Everybody knows it's only a matter of time, it's not your fault, they were coming anyway. Don't beat yourself up about that or anything. Just take it easy, unwind, ask them not to give you too much medicine. I'm going to make sure they tell us where you are, and I'm going to come see you and bring you whatever you need. Okay, Buddy?"

Deadly was a broken man. I walked him out with my arm around his waist. A guy in a suit came up and said, "I'll take it from here, I'll ride with you in the ambulance, Dudley. My name is Winters."

I watched the ambulance slowly head west.

Rick and Andy came over and we traded niceties. They wanted me to go to the Ranger Lodge and have a beer. I told them I was drained, just going to go crash at the El Cap campground with some hippie friends.

Talbot came over. He said, "Good job, man. Who do you work for?"

I gave him a CIA *coullion* look and thought about it; who do I work for? Only God knows.

I got in the Turtle, and the radio was playing some Quicksilver, a new song "Have Another Hit of Fresh Air." Finally, fresh air on the air, I thought, hope it's not too late.

Chapter 14

Climbers

The sun had gone down past the cliffs and we were in the last hour of daylight. I lay on my bedroll in the climbers' campground looking up the flat face of El Capitan. It is a massive granite mountainside, hard and slick rock. Two lunatics were strung together about three-quarters of the way up. Every now and then each would squirm like a sleepy caterpillar and twist and ping something a few times, hammering it into the rock. Then the rope would be repositioned and first one caterpillar and then the other would crawl up a few more feet... the ultimate *coullions*.

Bob came over and joined me looking up. "I'm gonna do that someday," he said.

"Been nice knowing you," I replied.

"Oh, it's not so dangerous once you know what you're doing."

"I'm sure. I think I heard that from my friend Thaddeus, the skydiver. Latest I've heard from him is how two of his best students drowned themselves by landing in the river. I have enough trouble with gravity as it is here on the ground."

"Mike, we heard what happened at the Headquarters, wanna talk about it?" Bob asked.

"Not really. Lucky somebody didn't get hurt. Good thing the Park Police weren't here yet, would've turned out badly, I'm sure. Of course now, with this and the riot the other night, it's inevitable, they'll be here soon," I said.

"So, how do you think things are gonna change?"

"I don't know, Bob, not for the better, certainly. I'd expect we won't be able to smoke openly, for starters. Probably start having searches of our vehicle, maybe even our camps."

"Can they do that without warrants?"

"Probable cause. They will say 'Your honor, this man had a psychedelic turtle painted on the side of his car so we knew he must have drugs inside it somewhere,' and the judge will probably agree, especially if they find or plant a stash."

"That's unAmerican, at least it doesn't sound like what we learned in school about the Constitution," Bob grumbled.

"The Constitution gets blurred when Washington or Baton Rouge gets paranoid and, boy, are they paranoid right now, got to hand it to y'all out here, your 'Revolution' has really gotten to them," and as I said that I noticed that I had begun distancing myself from the Plan.

"Thanks, but we don't want it to backfire, we're looking for more freedom, not less," Bob said, not aware that he had quickly drawn me back into the revolution by reminding me of freedoms already lost.

I was still staring up at the guys on the side of the world. "I don't think they can possibly make it to the top before dark. Do they climb with flashlights or what?"

"No, they're going to sleep up there and start again in the morning."

"Sleep hanging in ropes? I can't even sleep in a bed sometimes," I shuddered.

"No, they set up something like hammocks, slung from things like nails they drive into the cracks in the rock, it's very secure."

"Yeah, I'll bet. And do they piss into bottles or what?"

Bob laughed. "That's what Sara told me to be sure to tell you. You are right where the spray might reach if it hasn't evaporated from the fall. I wouldn't worry about it though. The drafts will swirl it around, might just take it over where we're set up, she's just uptight about it for some reason, like maybe she saw something she shouldn't have been watching."

I looked at him, gritted my teeth, got up and moved my bedroll back away from the base of the cliff. Besides, I told myself, I would hate to be sleeping and have a lunatic come crashing down on me.

Sara had some kind of barley soup ready. It was delicious.

She said, "I see that you've moved your bedroll. I'm glad."

"Yeah, thanks, I should've thought of that myself."

Bob said, "Once they've got themselves in their cocoons, we'll turn up the volume, didn't want to distract them while they were doing the technical stuff."

"What station is that?" I asked.

"It's AM, from Oakland, can't really get the FM behind these cliffs."

"Nice song, what group is this?" I asked.

"It's the Dead, good huh?" Bob said.

"Very good, what do you mean The Dead? Is that really what they call themselves?"

"The Grateful Dead. They're from the Bay Area, but they play a lot all over now."

I listened carefully. They sounded more conventional, more basic rock and roll than the other Bay Area groups, but they still had the strong, spacey, cantilevered psychedelic sound.

Sara added, "Perry says The Dead are going to be in Fresno two weeks from Saturday. He wants everybody there. He says we need to go in a couple of days early to get things 'primed.'"

So, that was the next step Perry had alluded to, a foray into the ultra-conservative center of the San Joaquin Valley.

I probed, "'Primed?' sounds like something is going to get pumped up."

"Most definitely," answered Bob. "We're going to turn 'em on and turn 'em loose!"

"Who?" I asked.

"The Valley kids, the ones under suppression by those old-fashioned people," Sara said with an uncharacteristically belligerent tone.

"You mean their parents?" I asked.

"Yes, and the school system down there, and their churches."

I could see the old-fashioned people cringing and getting even more certain that an evil Communist conspiracy was licking its chops about to devour their three little pigs. Was it?

Bob and Sara were, by now, used to my taking a devil's advocate position but I figured I'd preface any "cop questions" with some reassurance: "Y'all know that I plan to do something like you're talking about, back home in Louisiana, when I think it's the right time, but there's something that worries me about 'priming.' Can we talk about that for a minute?"

"Sure," both of them said at the same time.

I began, "I presume you intend to somehow get the Valley kids to go to the concert *en masse*?'

"Yes, that won't be too hard to do, it's a big arena, but we think it'll sell out. They've heard the Dead on the radio for a couple of months."

"And I suppose you plan to get as many of them stoned as possible for the concert?"

"Yes, Perry's ordered plenty, mostly grass. The Hell's Angels are bringing that up, then we're going to saturate any way we can everything within a fifty mile radius of Fresno, like from Hanford to Merced, from Coalinga to Coarsegold. We think we have enough contacts to spread out the entire donation."

"Sara," I asked, "suppose you were a parent and you found out that some people were going to give your daughter a bunch of dope and encourage her to go party with a bunch of out-of-town musicians?"

She tilted her head forward like she was looking at me over a pair of spectacles. "What?" she asked.

I tried to be more clear. "Don't you think that there's a risk that such a mass turn-on might have some unintended consequences? I mean, up to now, haven't y'all been sort of like shepherds, turning people like me on but being there for me, guiding me, helping me adjust while I learn? What's going to happen if some kid gets stoned with no mentor?"

Bob and Sara seemed reflective. Bob finally spoke. "Mike, it is true, what you say. We have been careful. I'd never thought of us like shepherds, but you are right. That's what we've been."

Sara shrank back a little saying, "I really think maybe you worry too much about things, Mike. That's what Alexis says."

I replied, "Maybe. Maybe not. I know that I've been on a couple of trips where I could have just about panicked if some of you hadn't been around to talk with me or just be there. It was very important to have someone steady with me. Maybe I should run this by Perry."

Bob said, "Yes, do that, can't hurt. See, Mike? We knew that you'd bring some extra perspective to the Plan! Make it stronger, make it bigger and better."

Yes, I thought, "Turn 'em on and turn 'em loose and who knows what might happen."

I asked "What do you suppose will happen at the concert in Fresno with all those first-trippers?"

Sara was getting back her gleeful nature, "Same thing that happened to you in the Avalon, Mike."

"Let's hope so," I said. "It wouldn't hurt if the musicians know what's going on."

"Oh, they know," exclaimed Bob. "Believe me, they know, and they've been figuring up the song sequence, all that stuff, they'll be very ready."

I slept fitfully. A couple of times I got up and walked over to the base of El Cap and looked up at the two cocoons hanging in the moonlight those hundreds of feet above me. How could tying oneself into a most precarious life-threatening optionless position be an expression of free will? Nuts, truly nuts, I thought.

Next morning I ate one of Bob and Sara's whole wheat biscuits with sheep butter and some kind of horrid tea. I told them I was going to make a quick run down to San Francisco to see The Wizards, Nathan, and Alexis but that I'd be back. I made sure they knew that Perry and Tim had some kind of summit meeting planned before the concert. I asked them to tell Perry that I planned to get the Wizards at least to the Dead concert in Fresno and that I'd like to go to the summit if I could. I asked them to be sure to run my "no-shepherds misgivings" by him if they saw him before I did. They said they'd tell him if they saw him.

I cranked up the Turtle and we headed downhill.

Chapter 15

Summits

Alexis was working an all-nighter. Nathan had the next 18 hours off, and he was ready to enjoy it lollygagging at his apartment with no intention of doing anything constructive, just resting. We kicked back and smoked a joint. He wanted me to see something on television.

"It's one of the public broadcasting stations here in the Bay Area," Nathan said. "Their nighttime news comes on at 9 P.M. instead of 10 o'clock or 11 like the other stations. See if you notice something weird."

We watched as an elderly, dignified, very conventionally-dressed anchorman plodded through some typical headlines in a very conventional, boring way. About four minutes into the broadcast, the man stated very matter-of-factly: "And, sources tell Channel 9 that because of the ongoing dispute over a lack of Black Studies courses at San Francisco State, a picket line will go up at 9:30 tomorrow morning at the corner of 19th and Holloway..."

With my peripheral vision I saw Nathan turn and look at me. I looked back at him with sort of a bewildered scowl. "Don't they have anything better to protest?" I asked. The anchorman went on with some other boring story. Nathan got up and turned off the television.

"Mike, tomorrow there will be a riot at that location. This station is calling the shots. When they embed a little statement like that in the 9 o'clock news, the organizers and the police know where to meet and duke it out."

"Oh, come on Nathan. You don't really think anybody would put something like that together, I mean, are you saying that the station is trying to foment civil unrest?"

"Exactly, and both sides support it. The radical leftists and the radical right. They have declared war on each other and they all want to escalate because they think it will get the apathetic American middle class activated on their side."

I figured Nathan was having a paranoid reaction to the grass he'd been smoking and I began to regret encouraging him to come to California. "Nathan, I think maybe the weed is distorting your perceptions."

"Now you, yourself, Mike, remember what you told me, 'This stuff might be the plant spoken of in the Book of Genesis, the Tree of Knowledge of Good and Evil.' You noticed that it helps cut through the deceit, it boosts insight, it opens up other cognitive dimensions. And you were right."

I had said all that. "Maybe I was wrong, Nathan. If it really is the Tree of Knowledge of Good and Evil, would I have to be saying 'might be' or wouldn't I just know for sure? I'm not sure, it might be some kind of super-complexifyer."

"What kind of word is that, Mike? You know this stuff cuts through the crap. Wait and see, riot tomorrow morning around 10 o'clock at 19th and Holloway!"

I'd stopped at Tower Records and bought the brand new Grateful Dead album. "Let's just listen to this, Nathan, supposed to be good and they're going to do a big concert in Fresno in a few days."

The album was excellent. Nathan brought out some leftover tuna fish casserole that Alexis had fixed the day before. "It's all she knows how to make except for cookie dough," he complained sadly, "and she eats that before she even cooks it. Definitely not a homebody." Nathan needed a homebody if anyone did. What did Alexis need?

"By the way," Nathan said, "I want you to meet one of the clerks from the hospital, her name is Marnie. I really like her."

So, the Universe was taking care of Nathan.

"Can she cook?" I asked.

Nathan smiled broadly and nodded, "Yes, she's a very good cook."

We watched the 10 o'clock news on another station. There was no mention of the impending riot at San Francisco State. Nathan turned the television off again. We listened to another album and drank some wine. At midnight he said, "Hold on a minute," and put on an FM station from Berkeley.

The DJ said, "News, picket line tomorrow at 9:30, 19th and Holloway, you know why."

"See, it's a pattern. I noticed it a couple of weeks ago and it holds up. The PBS station at 9 and this FM station at midnight, the word goes out."

I quit trying to argue against it. "If you say so, but don't you wish we could get people back home that organized? I mean: anything to shake them out of that inertia that the carpetbaggers and scalawags count on."

"Yes, things need to change at home, definitely. The longer the corruption lives, the stronger it gets. They've got everybody down there thinking like beggars, acting like beggars, and that state has more natural wealth than any other state in the country for its size."

Nathan was right about all of that.

"Suppose we were going to lay out some kind of a plan, Nathan, how to build a bridge from where things are to where they should be back home. Where would we start?"

Thus began our own little summit, a planning session that would actually change history back home across the years. We put together that night a long-term strategy. We thought in concepts, and we thought in details. We imagined best cases and worst cases. We drank no more wine, just coffee.

"Let's start by smoking another joint," said Nathan.

"Right, let me roll it out of my stuff. I've mixed in some blonde hash," I said.

"Why's it called blonde" he asked.

"It comes in sort of a smushy mass, softer than the black hashish, lighter in color, got a slightly different aroma. I think its smoother, a more mellow trip, my favorite."

Almost jokingly we came up with a "Let the bastards freeze in the dark" concept that eventually ended up on bumper stickers back home. Nathan mentioned it to his father in a phone call. His father, a friend of

Governor Edgard passed it on as a serious thought, not a joke. Edgard pushed the concept that the rest of the nation owed Louisiana for their warmth and electricity since the oil and natural gas either came from or came through the state. There was inherent in the bumper sticker slogan, of course, the implied threat of sabotage, disruption of the extensive, interconnected pipeline network. What Nathan and I had considered sort of a cutesy, snotty, childish remark other--powerful--people had adopted with a truly-malicious attitude.

Another one of the detailed, localized lines of action we envisioned that night was a way to replace the existing sheriff's dynasty. In the twentieth century, as sheriff in our home parish, there was just one family's man always "elected," father, son, grandson... That had led to some abuse of power. Our plan was to get a young policeman to run for city marshal when the old marshal was ready to retire. The new man would take the placid office up a level from serving summons and nailing up condemned building placards to also doing patrol work, motorist assistance, any law enforcement activity that normally would be done by the Parish Sheriff's Department or City Police. It would be touchy, but since those agencies were always undermanned there would be times when a marshal's patrol car could answer a call more quickly than could any other agency's units. As long as the marshals understood that they were to play the role of supplemental street police, and always defer to the existing hierarchy, gratitude rather than resentment should prevail. Then, the new marshal, after a couple of terms, could challenge the old, entrenched sheriff, or maybe make a deal for the old man to just retire gracefully and let the marshal be promoted to sheriff.

Pipe dreams, we had plenty of them that night and were still at it after daylight when Alexis came dragging in with edematous ankles from having been on her feet for over 20 hours straight. Worse than that, she'd obviously been crying.

Nathan saw that and went over, put his arms around her and said, "What's the matter, Doc?"

"We lost him, the one with that weird immune problem... We tried so hard..."

"Hello, Alexis, I'm sorry about whatever happened," I said feeling awkward and helpless.

"Hi, Mike, thanks..." She headed for the bathroom.

I told Nathan that I'd better leave, let them talk shop and get some rest.

"Okay," he said but seemed to want to explain something.

"Mike, this immune thing she mentioned, it's very peculiar. Nobody's ever seen anything quite like it. There have been several cases, all male homosexuals. Nothing seems to stop the progression, they just get sicker and waste away, develop a weird cancer or bacterial or mold infection and just die."

"Sounds bad, good thing it's just in a small group."

Nathan corrected: "Not such a small group, not out here."

I left and drove the Turtle over to the Mission District squatters. I noticed William's van parked down the street. Thaddeus and Donnie were awake but Mongoose, Terry, and Mark were well zonked out from whatever they'd been up to the night before.

"Hello, Thaddeus, Donnie. How's it going?"

Donnie answered, "It's okay. How are you?"

"Tired, up all night with Nathan, talking about home, need to change some stuff back there," I said.

"Yep. Long overdue but still too early," Thaddeus said wisely, "Place couldn't handle the kind of stuff that's happening out here."

I nodded agreement and added, "Neither can this place I'm afraid."

Thaddeus handed me a cup of coffee. Donnie went back up to his loft.

I told Thaddeus about the fantasies Nathan and I had developed overnight. He got into them and added a few twists.

"What time is it?" I asked. Thaddeus was one of the few people still wearing a watch and caring about punctuality.

"10:15."

I told him that Nathan had prophesied a riot to be taking place about then in San Francisco at State College based on a delusion that the news media were acting as controllers or coordinators of a bipartisan agreement to escalate civil unrest.

"Let's see," Thaddeus said. He went over and turned on an old police radio he had hooked up to a car battery next to his coffeemaker.

"Where'd you get that?" I asked while the tubes were warming up.

He didn't answer, just fiddled with knobs. It crackled and sputtered and we heard, "Tear gas ... running... rocks thrown... bottles... "

"Sounds like Nathan was right," observed Thaddeus nonchalantly. "Guess I'll have to get a TV. What station does he watch?"

We listened to the police deal with the mini-riot at San Francisco State. The demonstrators were dispersed. The various police were trying to outdo each other at sounding routine. There were three arrests, no injuries. Might make the 9 o'clock news, probably not 10 o'clock,

"I saw William's van down the street. What's the latest with his and Kenny's draft situation?"

Thaddeus spoke with satisfaction, "Lady at the Draft Board put the fear of God into them about that Conscientious Objector bullshit, let them know that they were facing jail time for lying. They could produce no evidence that they had ever even been in a congregation where there were real conscientious objectors. Their physicals have been rescheduled. Meanwhile, I'm still not letting them sleep in here, not till I'm convinced they've straightened out."

"You think they might still resist?" I asked.

"Kenny knows he cannot pass the physical, he's just going along with William, or maybe a better way to put it would be egging William on. I can't tell if it's because he truly wishes he had the physique to be a real draft resister himself, you know, a chance to be part of a 'revolution,' or just wants to be entertained by watching William screw himself."

"So, if Kenny weren't around, you think William wouldn't have put up any resistance?"

"Not sure, it's sort of too bad, he needed to find something to focus on, some kind of goal. He needed to start growing up, but he picked the wrong thing. He's made one mistake after another and doesn't even see them yet."

I thanked Thaddeus for the coffee and headed back to the Turtle.

William was climbing sleepily out of his van. I went over.

"Hey, William, how's it going?"

"Hey, Mike. It's okay. Heard about the Dead concert? They're going to be in Fresno. We're part of a caravan, nine vehicles so far, all loaded if you know what I mean."

"I know. I plan to be there myself, coming down from Yosemite. From what I hear, concert's going to be sold out as soon as the tickets go on sale. I've got to remember to talk to Sara. She knows how to ..."

"We've already got ours lined up, donated, along with a kilo. Man, this place is something. We need to do this kind of thing back home."

"Yes, we need to do something, certainly. Nathan and Thaddeus and I have been talking about that."

Kenny was climbing out of the van. "Hi, Mike. Peace."

"Hi, Kenny. Peace. I hear your physicals have been rescheduled."

"Yeah, this time we've got 'em. Got the evidence. No way we're going to let them send us off to fight the rich man's war," Kenny preached.

"What evidence?" I asked. William was looking suddenly very uncomfortable.

"Show him the pictures, William," Kenny pushed. William was hesitant.

"Okay, I'll get them." Kenny reached back into the van and brought out a stack of Polaroid snapshots. "Take a look," he said proudly.

I was more than disgusted, I was shocked. The pictures showed each of them engaging in homosexual acts.

"Yeah," I said. "That ought to do it. No Nam for y'all. No Louisiana either once this gets out. All I can do is pray for you." I looked at William who was looking at the ground in silent shame. I shook my head in profound and sincere disappointment and left.

I pondered what I could or should do about William and Kenny and decided that prayer was about the only thing that might have any positive effect, so I prayed.

On the drive back to Yosemite I made up my mind to begin extracting myself from the California scene and concentrate on repatriation, on going home for the bridge-building mission of all missions. Besides, I told myself, it looks like this scene out here is going bad, headed for self-destruction; maybe the thing to do is to gather up some seeds and get out before the field catches fire.

At the El Capitan campground I asked Sara if she could get us tickets in advance of the sellout. "Already done, Mike. Tim and Perry got a block of a hundred and fifty donated. All of us, rangers and naturalists if they want to go, trail crew, fire control aides, hotel workers, climbers, all of Yosemite is going, Fish Camp, too, shutting it down for the night so they can go."

"So, you've been in touch with Perry. Did you tell him of my misgivings, the shepherdless turn-on thing?"

"Yes," said Bob. "He understood but says there isn't much choice now, better to turn on a large group to grass immediately, risks or no risks, than to let the speed freaks take over."

I could see some logic in that, but more wishful thinking than good sense. "Did he say anything about the summit meeting?"

"Yes, he said to tell you the time and place are going to be agreed upon tomorrow, that you need to get to Wawona, he'll fill you in. I'd like to go with you. Sara wants to go to the City to talk with Alexis. She's going to hitch a ride down there with some of the climbers."

"Okay. Let me go see if anyone will tell me where they took Dudley. I need to know which VA hospital they put him in so I can go see him like I promised. I'll be back in an hour or two."

At Park Headquarters I spoke with Ranger Andy Anderson. He said that nobody knew yet where Dudley had been taken but he'd send word down to Stan Kelly as soon as he found out. He thanked me again for helping defuse the situation and I thanked him for probably holding off the FBI sniper I suspected might have been in the wings. Andy revealed, "Yes, he was here. Nice man. He was in no rush to go to work. How he could have been so calm facing that kind of job I don't know. He seemed as glad as anybody when it was over."

Scary, scary, I thought. What is it in the human mind that lets us deal with any circumstance? No, not everyone can deal with any circumstance; some people can't deal with the simplest of tests. One who can deal with having to be a sniper might not be able to deal with a fractious child. A mother who can deal with ten kids at once might not be able to deal with one bill collector. Still, there seems to be at least one human every time who can deal with anything that comes up on earth, maybe not right away but in time. I need to take a break from all this overstimulation I thought. I'm thinking too much, I need to go away, to some beautiful, quiet, peaceful place... and I realized that I was there, physically there, mountains, the tremendous waterfalls, peaceful, steady giant tree beings... how had I become detached from that reality and drawn into realities only in the human mind? Scary, scary.

I told Sara of the hard time Alexis was having dealing with the loss of one of her first patients, that she needed a friend, for sure. Bob and I took the Turtle up out of the Valley and headed toward the summit, the roadway summit. We stopped in the overlook to stretch our legs and watch another beautiful sunset, unstoned. A family of American tourists was doing the same. Would those children grow up to be drafted? I wondered if Bob were wondering the same thing. We got back in the Turtle and made it into Wawona.

At Perry's we found Elena and Tim making phone calls. She reached Chavez and invited him to the summit. He told her to handle it, report back to him. Tim called someone back east who promised he'd catch a flight that evening. Elena took another turn at the phone and got ahold of her father in Santa Cruz, asked him to find one of her friends and have her call back collect, night or day. Things were obviously in high gear.

Tim told us that Perry would be in shortly, for us to make ourselves at home. I took a shower and then a nap. Bob came to wake me up. "Perry's here. We're going to brainstorm."

Perry told us that the summit was set for the following afternoon at Fish Camp. People were coming from Los Angeles, Fresno, the Bay Area, Oregon, Ann Arbor, and the East Coast. Some were professors, some were "revolutionaries" of different sorts, there would be certain musicians, a couple of people involved in the movie industry, two or three representatives of "the national news media," the Hell's Angels, on and on...

"Perry," I asked, "That sounds more like a convention than a summit. How do you expect to accomplish anything with so many different Chiefs and no Indians? You know everyone's going to want to interrupt each other to get his or her cause made top priority."

"I realize that, but all we have to accomplish is to get each of those interest groups to remember that they are part of something bigger, something massive, nationwide, growing and powerful, ready to blossom and take America back over for the people. That's all we have to accomplish, just put them all together and flip the switch, the lights will go on, they will get back to where they each came from, and they will build their own bridges, crossing the same gorges that they know we all have to cross. We just have to emphasize the themes: love, peace, power back to the people."

Somehow, next day, riding down to Fish Camp lying in the back of Murphy's hearse, looking up but avoiding looking at the one giant star, the one too bright to see, its light wiping out all the other stars, somehow I felt centuries older and less wise than I had on any of the nocturnal hearse rides. How, I wondered, could cold little starlights be more comforting than the big warm illumination of the sun? I closed my eyes and tried to remember the synchronizations. Murphy didn't have any tape in the player. He, Bob, Zack, and Jim were just talking, serious things, unsynchronized..

Neither would the summit be synchronized. All that afternoon I said almost nothing. Also silent were The Pike and The Horsewhip. I wondered if they recognized me from the night they were throwing the kid off the bridge in Yosemite Valley. Maybe they were wondering if I recognized them, but they showed no signs of worry, about me or anyone else, mainly just signs of boredom. Yet they listened. I listened. Bob listened. Leo and Lena listened wondering if their Fish Camp would someday go down in history or just up in flames.

Elena plead that it was imperative that the plight of migrant workers be made a national issue. A Black Panther argued that a larger population group had been oppressed for a longer time and would have to rise up and take control of its own destiny whether anyone else supported it or not. A Bay Area musician who was also a student at San Francisco State begged the other musicians to take up the cause of the Earth and its living systems saying that one thing we could all do is demand a national ecology holiday.

A member of the Students for a Democratic Society bitched that San Francisco State needed to get its jock/eco-freak/ROTC head out of the sand and join the real world. A guy who looked like a hermit, like he could have been old Peyote Tom's father, reduced everything to one word, survival, survival of the individual, of the species, survival of civilization. The only one who mentioned the Great Spirit was the only Native American in attendance.

One after another, just as I'd told Perry I thought would happen, the Chiefs tried to recruit the Indians. Perry complimented each one and built a bridge to the next one, making sure everyone got to cover and recover his or her favorite point, while gently, almost subliminally, repeating his points of peace, love, and power back to the people. I admired his skills as a diplomat and psychologist. He was a master organizer. If he had any flaw it was in having set impossible goals for himself and for the "revolution."

Perry brought the summit to a close with an invitation to everyone to attend the Fresno Grateful Dead Concert. He had tickets for those who would be able to go, and extra ones for as many guests as they thought they could round up. He explained that we were "going to turn them on and turn them loose." He recommended that everyone do the same thing back home, wherever that was.

As I was walking back to the hearse The Pike and Horsewhip came over. "Where were your buddies?" Horsewhip asked.

"Who do you mean?" I asked, sincerely ignorant.

"The Rangers," Pike scowled.

"Oh, you know they wouldn't be able to come to something like this, even off duty."

"You off duty or on?" asked the Pike.

I was again surprised by the question but figured he took me for a cop.

"I'm not a cop if that's what you mean," I said.

"Don't matter if you are or you ain't," said Horsewhip, "you'd better watch your step because we sure are watching, whatever you're up to. That was our buddy Deadly you sent back to the hospital."

Murphy, Bob, Zack, and Jim walked up just as I was going to try to explain what had happened to Dudley. The Pike told them, "Watch out for this guy, he'll have you in a strait jacket if he gets his way."

Then the Hell's Angels got on their hogs and blasted away my next week's peace and quiet.

Zack said, "What did you say to set them off, Mike, what are they talking about?"

"Misunderstanding, they think I'm the reason Dudley is back in the asylum."

"Crap," Murphy, a man of few words, said it best.

Zack said, "I'll ask Perry to straighten that out if he can. Didn't you explain about the sniper in the tree?"

"Didn't get the chance," I said forlornly.

We got into the hearse. The sun set behind a peak, then rose out of a valley, then set behind another peak. It was dusk when we got back to Wawona, so again I had missed the stars. Murphy dropped me off at Perry's. As I walked the path to the house, I heard someone following me. I turned. There was no one there. I turned and began walking again. Again I heard someone walking, this time in front of me. I stopped. Insanity? Too many drugs? I opted for the Wawona Phantom and walked right through it to the house and crashed in a state of total fatigue and bewilderment.

Chapter 16

The Dead Concert

Jolie Blonde said it was something astrological: Everybody was going to be free the night of the Fresno concert. Nathan, Alexis, Zack, Jim, Ranger Rick, Betty, all had managed to get their days off changed or someone to cover for them. That did seem cosmic. It was obvious that Fresno was going to be invaded by not only the heaviest heads in the Revolution, but the freshest and most natural ones.

Bob, the Turtle, and I went down to San Francisco. I took Bob to Sara's then picked up Thaddeus, Nathan, and Alexis. Thaddeus was in a mood indigo and had refused to ride in William's VW van with the other Wizards. William, Kenny, Mongoose, Terry, Donnie, Mark, and some new Wizard groupies were jammed into the van. We headed up to Yosemite to pick up Peyote Tom and Jolie Blonde. Bob and Sara organized the caravan from Marin County. Zack and Jim had Big Roy, Snap Bean, and the Lieutenant in the old white Chevy. Murphy had Elena, Thin, and a couple of other hotel workers in the hearse. Perry and Tim had left three days early with one of Tim's professors. They were one of several "advance parties" making sure the "donations" (grass and tickets) were being well-distributed.

"What's bothering you, Thaddeus?" asked Alexis.

He didn't want to talk about it.

"How's it going with The Wizards?" asked Nathan.

He didn't want to talk about it.

I changed the subject, I thought. "Anybody hear anything from home, lately?" I asked.

Thaddeus opened up, "Damn Dunn, somehow heard that Alain is out here. He's coming to get him, and that damn little Kenny, got himself and William being investigated for sending pornographic materials through the mail, idiots, dumbasses, *coullions*... I don't know why I even tried..."

"Whoa, slow down," said Nathan. "What do you mean pornography through the mail, and how did Dunn find out about Alain?"

"They sent some pictures of themselves to the Draft Board figuring to get out of the draft because they now claim to be perverts."

Alexis, ever naïve, asked, "What do you mean perverts, what kind of pictures?"

Thaddeus could barely explain. "Actually, they did pervert themselves, for the sake of the pictures. I mean the pictures are real, they are really perverts. They'll get out of the draft easily now because they are going to jail for being morons."

Nathan said, "Well what about Mark... Alain... how'd Dunn find out, and does he have jurisdiction out here?"

Thaddeus said, "All he has to do is get one local cop to go with him, bust Alain, and they'll extradite him back home, thirty years. I don't know how he found out."

I asked, "Well, Mark's with William, in the van right now, on the way to Fresno, right?"

"Yes, I didn't tell them what I've heard. I'm still trying to figure out what to do. I didn't have time to set up some other escape. I figure Dunn, even if he shows up in San Francisco tonight, won't catch up to us all till tomorrow. Let the kid have one last night of freedom, maybe I can come up with something, got to be something I can do."

"Thaddeus," said Nathan, "you take too much responsibility for those kids on yourself all by yourself."

"Right," said Alexis, "we'll think of something."

For miles we were silent, remembering the sadist Dunn who used his badge to get his pleasures. Alain had not been the only childhood friend of ours to, with a relatively juvenile mistake, have stimulated Dunn's wrath and to have then suffered even corporal punishment.

After we picked up Jolie and Tom the conversation returned to Alain's predicament and the threat he was facing from the sadistic deputy.

Peyote Tom said, "I've seen cactus do wonders for that kind of person."

Everyone was quiet, trying to grasp what sounded like a complete absurdity.

I said, being as gentle as I could, "Tom, Dunn would never agree to a peyote trip."

Tom said, "He will if the Universe decides that's the best thing to happen."

Thinking aloud I suggested another plan: "Maybe we could have the Trail Crew hide Mark back in the wilderness..." and Thaddeus completed the plan:

"And we could send Dunn up after him and let Snap Bean do an intercept..."

What in the world were we doing, unstoned? We had progressed from peace planning to having a trained killer ambush a cop in the backwoods. I said, "Nathan, roll us a joint, please."

I turned on the Turtle's old AM radio and tuned into the Fresno station. The DJ that sounded like my friend Casey from back home was playing one Grateful Dead song after another hyping the concert.

We did a quick round in Wawona to see if everyone was set up for the trip down to Fresno. Stan Kelly was sitting in his patrol car at the Pioneer History Center talking with Karl. I pulled the Turtle up. "Hi, Stan. Hi, Karl. How's it going?"

"Fine, Mike. Looks like you've got a carload there, going to the concert like everyone else?" Stan asked.

"Yes, that's where we're headed. Looks like most everyone else is ahead of us."

"They've been leaving for days, getting mighty quiet up here," smiled Karl.

Stan took a paternal tone and said, "You all be careful down there, stay out of trouble."

"We plan to stay way out of trouble," said Alexis.

Continuing with his tone of admonition, Stan said, "Mike, give me a call if you need anything, day or night. When can we expect you back?"

I thought about that. "I'm not sure, Stan. We might find a place to stay in Fresno after the concert, or maybe I'll take Thaddeus, Nathan and Alexis right on back to San Francisco. I'd imagine that Jolie, Tom, and I should be back in the park within a few days at the most, maybe even tomorrow, just depends."

"Well, again, be careful," he warned, and gave me a look as if he knew something he couldn't talk about.

I nodded that I was getting the extra message. "Thanks, Stan. Hope to see you soon."

We headed out of the park. Jolie said, "Aren't all the Rangers so nice? They seem to really care about people." She was right. I mulled over what would likely happen once the Park Police would arrive. Maybe the Rangers could keep their image and public trust, maybe not.

Alexis inquired, "Mike, that Ranger seemed to me to be more than a little worried. Was that my imagination?"

"No, Alexis, very perceptive. He was giving me a silent supplement to what he could say aloud."

"What do you mean," asked Nathan.

Thaddeus was reading my mind and guessed, "I'll bet Dunn has been making calls to the Rangers like he was to the SFPD." I wondered if Captain Ross had been the one who, through Perry, had tipped Thaddeus about Dunn.

"Only other two things it could be," I theorized, "is that the Park Police are going to have some kind of advance party undercover at the concert or else law enforcement has been tipped that some kind of altercation is planned, like what happened with the Hell's Angels at the river."

Jolie Blonde squirmed, "Definite worryworts, all of you. Sara was right."

Tom blandly said, "Leave it all in the hands of the Universe; that's where it is anyway."

We silently left it there since that's all we could do at the time.

As we got to the flatland vineyards and orchards, we saw Elena's many amigos sweating under the lowering sun, picking our luxury foods for us. We made what these days would be called "politically-correct" commiserations and kept on driving into Fresno. Since we still had plenty of time before the concert we found a small restaurant for supper. The people in the restaurant became wary when we walked in and kept us under observation the entire time. The waitress seemed almost afraid of us. As I was paying our bill on the way out, the owner asked "Here for the big concert?"

"Yes, sir." I answered. The "sir" seemed to surprise him. He just gave me my change and we left.

Nathan said, "That guy looked like he wanted to grill us."

Tom said, perceptively, "As in on a spit?"

Alexis tried to get everyone back onto the same verbal level. I asked a kid in the parking lot the best route to the Sports Arena. When we got there, traffic was already bad. I decided to drive on past the place and park about five blocks away in a quiet residential neighborhood. "This will give us time to walk in, smoke a joint on the way, keep the Turtle out of the confusion" I explained.

Alexis protested, "Smoke out in the open while we are walking?",

Jolie Blonde answered, "Oh, Doc, quit worrying, we do it all the time."

Nathan reinforced Alexis, "You do it all the time in the park and in San Francisco, but I hear that this place is ultra-conservative."

"Tell you what," I said. "We won't start smoking until we're away from the car, that way the nearest neighbors won't be able to tell the cops anything except that they saw us walking."

"What about the other neighbors down the road?" asked Alexis.

"By the time the cops get to us, we'll be at the arena, blended into the throng," I said.

"And blended into all the other smoke," said Thaddeus.

We left the Turtle and about a block later Jolie lit up, Thaddeus lit up, and I lit up. We were passing three joints among five people. By the time we got to the arena even Alexis and Nathan were laughing. Okay, I told myself, just relax and have a fun night. I did notice sprinkled in the crowd both outside and inside the arena uniformed policemen and Hell's Angels, in about equal numbers.

"We'd better have a plan, in case we get separated," mothered Alexis.

We set up the plan, worst case, meet up back at the Turtle at midnight.

Thaddeus suggested that we split up immediately and try to find everybody else and meet soon at some predetermined location. We looked around and decided to meet at the first section of seats above the arena's floor. From that spot we would have a good view of the stage, which was set up only slightly lower than our ledge. We could also watch the people on the floor and turn to see the rest of the huge crowd in the seating area.

Nathan, Alexis, Tom, and I took some seats, leaving others between us, saved for Thaddeus, Jolie, and anyone else we might find. Nathan said, "Hey, there's Perry." I got up, went down the steps onto the floor and out to talk with Perry. He assured me with a great grin that all was well. I told him I was glad but that we'd had word that a parish deputy was on his way to grab Alain. Perry did not seem surprised but said, "Would you recognize the cop if he shows up here tonight?"

"Sure, we all would," I said.

He motioned for someone to come over. Two came, the Horsewhip and the Pike. Perry explained the situation. Then he told me, "If you see the cop, get these men's attention and then go shake hands with the cop. Then go back to your seat. It'll be taken care of, understand?"

I was afraid to understand, but I nodded, "Thank you. All of you."

The Horsewhip and The Pike smiled at me. Their previous hostility seemed to have evaporated. I supposed that Perry must have told them how I'd gotten Deadly out of the sniper's line of fire.

Perry asked, "Now where is Alain?"

"I don't know. Thaddeus is trying to find him and the other Wizards right now."

"As soon as you can, point out Alain to these men so they know who the target is and can keep an eye on him." I didn't like the sound of that, but I agreed and went back up to my seat to wait for Thaddeus.

The Pike and Horsewhip moved around the stage continuously, going up onto it, backstage, back down in front, critically controlling the whole stage zone as if they were the Secret Service protecting the President.

"Here they come," Tom announced. We all looked around and saw only strangers.

Half a minute later Jolie said, "Oh, there they are."

Nathan, Alexis, and I still saw only strangers. Peyote, I realized then, was at work with its early awareness of approach. Neat. The universe was giving Tom and Jolie to each other and to all of us.

Finally I saw Thaddeus coming through the crowd, followed by Mark, Mongoose, Terry, William, Kenny, and their groupies. Crossing from a different direction we saw Zack, Jim, the Trail Crew, Murphy, Elena, Thin, and the other hotel workers. They all ran into each other and Thaddeus led the whole bunch up into our seating section. Thaddeus told Alain/Mark to sit in the middle of everyone else.

"I haven't told them yet, about Dunn," Thaddeus said to me. I told him of the setup with the Hell's Angels and that we'd need as many of us as possible on the lookout for Dunn. "Right," he said, "guess it's time to put them on alert." He did that and the Wizards all muttered dejectedly among themselves. I caught Horsewhip's attention. I then put my hand on Mark's shoulder. Horsewhip nodded that he understood who we were protecting from disaster.

The arena was overflowing with people and grass smoke. Dozens of police from different agencies were nervously watching but making no moves to bust anyone obviously having been told not to set off some kind of riot. A line of tough-looking police moved up against the lower front of the stage, placing themselves between the stage and the kids wanting to have the closest look at the musicians. Horsewhip and Pike made their way along that line of cops, first on the floor and then just above them on the apron of the stage, saying nothing, just looking each cop in the eye for a moment.

I scanned the crowd. Far up above us on the last row of seats I saw Rick and Betty. They had apparently already been watching us. I waved for them to come on down. Rick waved me up. I went. He told me that he and Betty needed to be as anonymous as possible. "We will just stay high, up here," Betty said with a mischievous grin. Grass or peyote or "natural high" or what was being called "contact high," I couldn't tell.

"Well, you naturalists, I'll expect a report on the ecology of this concert on my desk in the morning," I said.

Rick smiled and saluted, "You've got it, Superintendent."

Roadies finished getting the equipment set up on the stage. Musicians began taking their places, and the crowd began to clap and cheer. Some tuning up took place and then what looked like Horsewhip's cubical twin, in a hippie costume, came on stage as the music cranked up and the crowd went nuts. "It's Pigpen," yelled Jolie Blonde, "it's him!"

He was singing a crude song "Good Morning, Little Schoolgirl, Can I Come Home With You?" and Jolie was screaming, "Yes, yes, yes!"

Wasn't that an old Willie Dixon blues song? I couldn't remember.

Alexis looked mortified. Nathan looked at her and burst out laughing. I hoped it was going to be a good night.

In the middle of the next song, Pigpen, suddenly stopped singing and waved for the Dead to stop playing. The place went dead silent.

He chided, "Come on, Fresno, you going to let these pigs intimidate you? What's the matter with you, come on up here, right to the stage, this is America, they can't keep you away from us, we're on our way and you're coming with us!"

The crowd cheered and pressed toward the stage. The row of cops pushed back for a few seconds then someone signaled them to peel off to the sides and disappear. While that was happening, The Wizards leaped over the railing onto the floor of the arena and joined the symbolic movement forward as did the Trail Crew, Jolie and Tom, and finally even Nathan, Alexis, and I. Naturally, everyone couldn't squeeze onto the arena floor and common sense prevailed. Pigpen sang a verse into the song, "Good work, you've done it, we're on our way together Fresno," or something like that and the crush relaxed. Some of us filtered back out of it and up to our seats. The music was great. There was a rudimentary kind of light show but I could see that big arenas could never allow duplication of the psychedelic intimacies that were possible in the Avalon.

Midway into another song, Peyote Tom stepped over to me, tugged at my arm and silently led me out into a corridor. He spoke into my ear, "Universe tells me to tell you to look around out here." I spotted Dunn with two uniformed policemen and a couple of cops in plain clothes. He had not seen me, yet. I told Tom to go back in and alert Thaddeus, that I was going to lead Dunn to the Horsewhip and the Pike.

I pretended not to see Dunn but after a couple of minutes I walked across his line of sight and back out onto the arena floor. I made my way through the crowd, glancing up to our seats. Thaddeus had hidden Alain. That was good. I pushed my way up to the stage and got the Pike's attention. I turned and walked back, seeing that Dunn and the cops had taken the bait. I went up and yelled over the music "Hey, Dunn, what are you doing here?" and put out my hand for a shake which he refused.

"Where's that little pusher? Is he here?" he bellowed.

I looked at the Fresno cops. "Who are you talking about, I thought you'd got over your paranoid collapse, Dunn, what are you talking about?"

He grabbed me by the shirt, fire in his eyes.

About then the Fresno cops pulled him back, motioning for him to look around. About seven Hell's Angels had moved in close to us. The Fresno cops jostled Dunn toward the exit. The Angels followed them at a distance. As they went out of sight, I looked up at Thaddeus. He was watching them like an osprey watches from its perch above a bayou. He turned toward me with a sudden smile and gave me a thumbs up. The Wizards all broke into cheers and clapping in the middle of the song. The other audience members nearby who could hear them gave them crazy looks and told them to stop interrupting the performance. Mark/Alain peered up from behind a row of seats. Big Roy pulled him up by his collar and got him back on his feet again. It was a good night.

Bridges had been designed and built. Peace, love, and power were coming back to the people. I thought to myself, "Perry, you've done it. It worked. If it can work in Fresno, it can work in Middle America. Maybe it can even work in Lake Charles, turn 'em on and turn 'em loose." And then I came back to my less euphoric common senses, "Wait and see, see how this plays out, no shepherds, who knows which direction this will take. Will it self-lead, will someone rise to the top and lead it, in the right direction, in the wrong direction, or will it just go into a stampede over the cliffs? No shepherds unless... The shepherds will have to be nationwide, news people, musicians, Hollywood, DJs... Not a chance... too far gone, ahead of the shepherds, the song is outrunning its melody."

Everyone else stayed euphoric for days. Thaddeus sent Alain into the wilderness with the Trail Crew. I briefly remembered the evil scenario we'd contemplated... I pushed it out of my mind again.

The Fresno Dead concert had changed everything, allied many groups on a high conceptual level, defused many potentially competitive or even adversarial interests, and had at least delayed a collapse of Perry's bridges.

I decided to give myself some private time, drive over to Reno, say hello to my cousins, play a few hands of blackjack, recalibrate.

Chapter 17

The Free Clinic

I watched a sunset across Tuolumne Meadows then left the park headed for my cousins' places in Nevada. The road east out of Yosemite was not the main route out of the park since it was tortuously crooked and going toward one of the least populated parts of the United States. I'd heard that there was a particularly hostile county policeman between the park boundary and the state line, one who disliked hippies with flowery paint jobs on their vehicles. Maybe he prefers turtles I thought positively.

Headlights fell in behind me and crept up to an unsafe distance. Tailgaters again, can't they see that this is a turtle and turtles are slow? I kept as constant a speed as I could on the slopes and hairpins, but the headlights stayed right on me. Then they went from dims to brights and crept right up to my bumper. As I rounded a tight curve, in my left door mirror I caught a glimpse of the side of the car behind the headlights. There was a police emblem of some type on its door. So, I thought, he doesn't like turtles either, why doesn't he just put on his red light and pull me over?

I was breaking no laws and he knew it, and I knew that he knew that I knew it. He was waiting for me to make a mistake. I considered it unconstitutional harassment and became angry. "Just what he wants," I told myself, "another Dunn." I reckoned that Dunn wouldn't let up until he'd gotten his way and neither would this guy. "How many miles to the state line?" I asked myself. After doing some mental calculations, I guessed I was getting within five miles of Nevada, maybe I'd make it.

The harasser also knew that his time was running out. He kept creeping up to within a yard or two of my bumper. I expected him to put on the red light at any moment and cook up some excuse for pulling me over. Impulsively I sped up like I was going to try to "rabbit" as I'd heard Thaddeus put it, run from the law, high speed chase they call it nowadays. He sped up too, but just as he was catching up I slammed on my brakes as hard as I could, then hit the gas as hard as I could. He reacted to my braking by slamming on his brakes but almost put himself over the cliff as I sped away. I slowed down a couple of miles later as I approached the state line. Way back up the hill I could see his headlights coming, red light spinning too.

As I crossed into Nevada a State Trooper unit was approaching. We passed each other and he turned around and fell in behind me. Unlike the county cop, the trooper followed me at a reasonable distance, all the way to the outskirts of Carson City where I pulled into my cousin Rosemary's farm. The trooper went on by slowly. It was late at night but Rosemary welcomed me in.

"Where have you been, boy? Everyone's been real worried. We haven't heard from you in weeks."

"Yosemite, mostly, and San Francisco, just taking it easy."
"You don't look like you're taking it easy, you look like hell."

She was right, too much stress, hadn't shaved in weeks, no haircut, and a hard night sweat from the ride down.

She took a short phone call. We had some wine and a long conversation. Then I took a shower and went to bed. Next morning I could hear her outside feeding her menagerie. I got up and was in the kitchen looking for coffee. Rosemary came in and said, "Don't look now, but I think you brought the cops with you. What have you done?"

I looked out the window and saw two State Trooper patrol units parked across the highway.

"Might as well go face the music," I said.

"Wait, I'll fix coffee first, tell me what's going on."

I told her. She said, "Well, I saw the psychedelic turtles on your car, can you blame the guy?"

"Yeah, I can blame him, what's the harm in some painted turtles?"

"He probably thinks you're a dope pusher. Are you?"

I gave her the CIA *coullion* look and went on out to the State Troopers.

"Hello, I'm Mike. I'm the driver of that old Buick. I guess y'all want to talk to me or something."

The troopers got out of their cars and asked for my identification.

One of them said, "You come over from Yosemite last night?"

"Yes, sir."

"Did you see a police car with its red light trying to pull you over up there?"

"As I was crossing into Nevada, way up behind me I did see a red light, not before that."

The other trooper asked, "What did you see before that, farther back?"

"A dangerous tailgater who stayed on my bumper for miles with his brights in my mirror. I tried to let him pass, but he wouldn't. I got scared. I thought maybe it was some kind of killer or something. I finally made a dash to get away from him."

The troopers looked at each other. One said, "Next time you see a red light in your mirror you'd better stop, understand?"

"Yes sir." I started to ask whether the cop with the red light had caught the killer, but I decided not to push my luck.

Rosemary had come out onto her porch to watch. The troopers waved at her and drove off. I went back to the house. "You know those guys?" I asked.

"Of course. One of them called me last night to see if I was okay or if you were some kind of hostage-taker. I have some paint thinner if you want to scrub that silly stuff off your car."

"No, thanks, I'm going to leave it, I like it, turtles on the Turtle. You like animals, why don't you like my turtles?'

"I like real turtles, not dope turtles."

"It's not about dope, it's about mental freedom."

"Sure, come in and have some pancakes."

I spent a couple of days at Rosemary's, then in Reno a couple of days at Gene and Betty's place, then in Portola at Aunt Willie Mae's. She prayed for me, even in tongues. At Billy's in Graeagle I watched the little kids ski. They said it was easy but I sensibly resisted their urgings that I try it. That branch of the family had moved out west, in the thirties, when the sawmills had finished raping the virgin longleaf pine forests at home. The lumber barons had not replanted, just gone on to the next set of old growth forests, Northern California. My uncle and his fellow lumberjacks and mill hands had followed. Even though they were now Californians they could still cook chicken and dumplings like my grandmother. They made me extremely homesick. Were these wonderfully unusual folks really representative of what was now being called "The Silent Majority?" I headed back to San Francisco re-grounded in my old roots.

Unfortunately I woke up Alexis when I got to their apartment. Nathan wasn't home.

"He and Marnie are volunteering at the Free Clinic in the Haight," she yawned.

"Go on back to sleep, I'm sorry I woke you up." She looked like she had something to tell me, but I insisted on leaving and letting her get her rest. She didn't press it.

I parked the Turtle on a side street, a rather steep hill. That always bothered me. It was a worry that we didn't have at home. I'd had to learn to "curb the wheels" so that the car would be less likely to roll out of control if the parking brake failed. I had to remember to pull the parking brake. New things to remember, one after another.

I walked up the narrow staircase in the old Victorian building. The upper floor had been converted into a makeshift clinic. A big semi-psychedelic poster announced "Speed Kills."

Kids were sitting around with forlorn looks, staring at the floor or ceiling, some fidgeting, some whimpering with their faces in handkerchiefs.

A young lady sitting behind a desk motioned me over and handed me a clipboard with a one-page form to fill out: Name, Address, Phone Number, Next-Of-Kin, etc. I told her I wasn't there as a patient, just wanted to see a friend of mine, Dr. Nathan. She said, "He's real busy right now, maybe you could just leave a message?" I said I would do that, and she directed me to "Just turn that same sheet over." When she read the note she said, "So, you're the Mike I've heard so much about. I'm Marnie."

I was touched. She must have fallen in love with Nathan and was already following him to the ends of the earth. "Hello, Marnie, I'm glad to meet you, and I'm especially glad that Nathan has met you." She seemed embarrassed but glad to hear that.

I continued, "You know that he's a champ but he needs somebody, he wants somebody to love if I could borrow a local phrase."

She seemed even more embarrassed and even more glad to hear that one.

"Let me know if I can ever, ever help you two," I said with all sincerity.

She sort of stammered "You...you grew up with Nathan and... Alexis... didn't you?"

I sensed the anxiety, the question in the word "Alexis" when she spoke it.

"Yes, we all were kids together, and we still are, all just lifetime good friends...that's what it is, just lifetime good friends..." I emphasized the "good friends" part enough that I saw her sigh in relief.

As I was leaving she gave me two brochures: "Speed Kills," and "How To Help the Free Clinic."

Noble idea, like the Free Store, I thought. Noble people, still trying to hang onto that special time that was slipping away so fast. I was very proud of Nathan. I told him that in the note.

I drove over to Perry's apartment. "Mike, come on in, where have you been? Things are happening." He seemed glad to see me but nervous.

"I've been up in Reno and Portola. What's happening?"

As I walked into the apartment I saw the Horsewhip and Pike toking on a bong.

"Well, for one, your sadistic deputy problem is over," crowed Horsewhip.

I had a combination of elation mixed with dread. "What do you mean, over?"

"Like lots of flatlanders, he overestimated his ability, took a fall from the Glass Rock Trail. Gets a tourist every other year on average. This was his year," smiled The Pike.

"Dunn's dead?" I figured I might as well ask.

Perry said, "Yes, dead, Snap Bean and the Lieutenant found him. Notified Stan Kelly. Stan went up, took pictures, then they carried him down. Found a gun in his new backpack."

"What was he doing up there?" I asked, knowing that he'd probably been tipped that Alain was being hidden by the Trail Crew.

The Horsewhip was grinning. "Now, Mike, you know tourists, they breathe the mountain air, get the bug, decide to go native, some of them make it work, some don't, it's just natural selection."

Peace and Love? Is that the grin of a loving person I asked myself. Peace? Is that the grin of a pacifist? At least Perry had a straight face. I looked at him with my thoughts and for the first time he turned away. Power? Yes, I guess the Horsewhip and the Pike were people who were grinning the grins of power taken back from the abusers. Nevertheless, power back to the wrong people... I shuddered, again.

"I guess Peyote Tom was right, the Universe handles things that need to be handled," I tried weakly to respond to what I'd heard.

"He's that old guy we almost drowned, isn't he?" asked Horsewhip.

I hadn't intended on bringing up some other stress. I kicked myself.

Perry picked it up, "Yes, he made it, though."

The Horsewhip carried on, "Like I said, natural selection, that's what the naturalists call it. If they're meant to make it, they will."

I was hoping the topic would drop, change, or something. It did.

Perry shifted the conversation. "Mike, since the summit and since Fresno, things are popping..." He went on to give me coast-to-coast updates while I took a reckless toke from the Angels' bong. Led Zeppelin was on the stereo.

Perry got back on Bay Area happenings and said, "Your little buddies William and Kenny got busted, Federal rap, unlawful use of the mail, sending pornographic materials, draft board has stamped them thoroughly unfit, how about that?" He seemed glad they'd succeeded in beating the system.

How about that, indeed. Idiots. I just took another toke and thought "Have to go see Thaddeus, he's probably having fits or washed his hands of them altogether. Guess that's the best thing to do."

Perry continued, "Your pal, Doc Nathan, is volunteering at the Free Clinic, good man, doing good things."

"Yes, I went by there awhile ago to see him, but he was too busy. I'll catch him at home."

The Pike asked, "See all the propaganda on the clinic wall about 'Speed Kills.?'"

"Yes, I saw that."

"Two sides to every story," Horsewhip threw in.

I was wondering how he planned to defend a drug that was taking down every bridge that had been planned and built so painstakingly.

"But that one, I have to agree," he choked out with half of his last toke.

"Yeah," he breathed. "It got a couple of our Angels. Got 'em good. Got to rethink that one. Maybe limit it to selected customers, natural selection assistance..." he trailed off.

I looked at Perry. My mind had begun to celebrate. "Man, either these guys have a lot more upstairs than I thought, or you, Perry, have put in a keystone in a critical arch, the Angels' bridge arch!"

Perry smiled. He was a master psychologist, a master organizer.

"Mike, Canned Heat is playing tonight at the Haight Theatre. The Angels have a neat surprise in store for us."

I figured I'd better get on over to Thaddeus's while I still could. "Sounds good. Let me go over to the Wizards, tell them. What time tonight?... Okay, we'll be there." I started to give the drowsy angels a salute but flashed them a peace sign instead. Pike flashed one back.

Thaddeus had already heard about the Canned Heat concert. He was moping about, kicking things, cussing in the abstract. I told him I'd heard about Dunn, and I'd heard about William and Kenny.

"Are they in jail?" I asked.

"Damn right, and I have a mind to let them rot there," he said but I detected a tone of fatherly mercy in his voice. Old habits die hard...

"What about Dunn, what do you think really happened?" I asked.

"Sounds like you think the same thing I think, better let it go at that," Thaddeus said and we did, permanently.

Thaddeus had the keys to William's van so we used that to go to the Haight. Before we went to the theatre, we went into what had been renamed from The Drogstore to Magnolia Thunderpussy's. Must've been taken over by rednecks, I figured. An even greater variety of people than before were inside, all planning. We had some coffee almost as strong as at home then walked on to the Haight Theatre.

Canned Heat aggravated the air with their hyperbolic electric rhythms and blues. I kept waiting for the Hells' Angels' surprise. Suddenly ripping down the aisle came two unmuffled Harleys, driven by Horsewhip and Pike, with naked women riding on the backs like Ladies Godiva! The four of them looked like they were in some kind of ecstatic orgasmic state, and maybe they were. They made a loop down to the old theatre's orchestra pit and then roared up the opposite aisle back to the lobby and back outside blistering their way up the hill toward Golden Gate Park.

The crowd was screaming and Canned Heat kicked in with another power song.

Yes, neat surprise, legendary.

"They missed it, they missed it," Alain was saying as he jumped up and down.

I guessed he was talking about William and Kenny.

The mellowness was gone. The peace was well-disturbed. The love was aging fast. The people were not, however, relinquishing their grasps for power. Even an ugly bridge might span an ugly canyon I realized. Maybe we can get across and maybe we can replant on the other side. I was trying hard to hope.

Chapter 18

Lookout Tower

Alexis and Nathan asked to borrow the Turtle for a weekend trip they'd been wanting to take, to see Muir Woods, Point Reyes National Seashore, and Bodega Bay. I planned to house sit their apartment for them, but Zack and Jim came into the City on their regular run. They suggested that I join them for the trip back up to Yosemite. Bob and Sara were up there but planning to come back down in a few days, so I would have a way back. I wanted to talk with the Trail Crew about Dunn and thank them for taking care of Alain. I left a note for Nathan and Alexis.

The trunk of the Chevy had its normal cargo. On the way up to the park on Zack's eight-track we listened to mellow, Bay Area groups only. Zack and Jim agreed that something was being lost, that we had indeed been privileged to have experienced it when we had since it might never come back. Jim said he was thinking of going back to Nebraska and just growing weed, fields of it mixed in with his corn crop for cover. He was concerned about an embargo that could come, running the price of grass up substantially. He said, sounding almost like a commodities trader, "I can see it going to $50 a kilo, maybe more. That would really put a damper on things."

Zack said, "No change for me. Just the park and San Mateo and the City. I'll always be able to slide over into a fun and comfortable niche."

I envied Zack. He did seem to have it knocked. We stopped in Modesto for gas and a hamburger.

The old Chevy made its turns on the government's back roads. As we approached the road that would have taken us up to Bernie's lookout tower, Zack slowed to a stop. "Damn," he said.

"What a pisser!" said Jim.

"What's the matter?" I asked.

"Trouble," Zack said as he turned the car around and headed back downhill.

"Signal, Bernie hung a towel on the north rail of the tower," explained Jim.

"What does it mean?"

"Means we have to bury the cargo," said Jim.

Zack pulled up to one of the steel gates to another fire road. Jim got out and unlocked it.

We drove in, Jim relocked the gate behind us. We drove in about a quarter of a mile.

The ground was rocky, and they had only one shovel, so we took turns digging a hole.

"I wonder if anyone will ever retrieve this buried treasure?" I asked, trying to lighten up the mood a little. They didn't respond.

We got back into the Chevy and made our way to Wawona. Zack pulled into the hotel parking lot. We went into the coffee shop. Elena looked flushed but steady. "Hello you guys," she said in a practiced normal way.

"Coffee all around, good to see you, Elena," I said.

"Pie?" she asked.

"Yes, that too," I said.

As she brought things to us she would whisper details of what had been happening:

"Park Police, they're here, all over the park. Must be dozens of them, white uniforms, old-fashioned cop hats. Busted Bernie, found one roach in his tower. But he saw them coming and got the signal out over the radio. So far they haven't found anything else, not one joint. Thin walked right past them out of the dorm carrying his potted pot plant and they did not even recognize it. They've searched everything, all the lockers, under the mattresses, everything."

Zack and Jim began to relax, even smile. "So, it worked!" Zack said exuberantly.

"Except for Bernie," Elena lamented. "Man, they'll probably throw the book at him, over one roach."

I asked, "I wonder why he didn't just pitch it over the side?"

"You have to know Bernie," she said. "For one thing he probably forgot it was there, may well have ditched his day stash and then got busy on the radio to save our butts, good old Bernie. He did it."

I asked another question, "You would think that if there were going to be a big raid that other places would have got hit simultaneously, I wonder why they hit his place first?"

Zack and Jim thought about that. Jim said, "Good question, maybe they messed up, got unsynchronized, or maybe they were figuring to creep up there and catch us with our load. We were a few hours later than usual."

Zack said, "All along, we figured that when a raid would come, at least one or two stations would have time to send out the coded notification, then the other stations would spread the word in their area, by phone or signals like Bernie did or just talking to key folks. It was all set up and it worked beautifully."

"I'll bet those new Park Police are livid. All their planning and they blew it," I said.

"Here they come again," warned Elena.

I turned and saw three uniformed officers coming into the coffee shop. They were not happy.

They came right over to us and one asked, "Whose old white car is that out there?"

Zack said, "Mine."

The cop ordered, "Let's go take a look."

Zack and Jim headed out with the cops.

I left money on the counter and followed them.

The cops were looking through the windows of the Chevy and asking questions.

Zack was answering each question, quickly but carefully. He must have been through this kind of thing before, I thought--glad I'm not in his shoes--not yet, anyway.

One cop finally demanded, "Open the trunk."

Zack said, "Got a warrant?"

The cops all pursed their lips and squinted.

One said, "You getting smart with us, hippie?"

Zack said, "No, just wondering if you've got a warrant. We've given you no cause to ignore the Constitution, have we?"

One of the other cops said, "I want to see your ID's, all of you."

We each produced our driver's license.

"San Mateo, Nebraska, Louisiana, what are you doing up here in the Park?" he asked.

"I'm a tourist," I said. "I like to hear the Naturalists' talks; they are very educational."

He scowled, "What about you, Nebraska, you a tourist, also?"

"No, I work here, seasonally, Fire Control Aide."

Zack said, "Same for me."

The third cop said, "Well, guess what fellows?" He pulled a document out of his jacket. "We do have a warrant to search this very Chevy; open it up smartass."

Zack complied cheerfully, "All I wanted to see was a warrant."

All the cops wanted to see wasn't there.

"Mind if I ask what you were looking for?" inquired Zack in contrived innocence.

"You know damn well and listen to me, boy, before this is over, your ass will rot in a cell."

The cops went back to their shiny new patrol car and drove off steaming.

"That went well," laughed Zack. Jim pulled a joint out of his pocket and lit up.

I felt shaky. "You had that on you all the time?" I asked. He grinned and passed it to me.

I took a toke and passed it to Zack who was also laughing. These guys are nuts, truly nuts, I thought.

We finished the joint and went back into the coffee shop.

"They had a warrant, Elena, for my car," said Zack.

"I saw that and I saw that you were lucky they didn't search your persons; you'd better be more careful from now on."

Zack and Jim became more serious. "We plan to, things have changed, we know that. More pie, please."

After the coffee shop, we were headed to Tim and Perry's place when Stan Kelly flagged us down. He got out of his official old green station wagon and asked: "Just coming back in?"

Zack answered "Yes, we had some coffee and pie at the hotel. Elena told us about the Park Police raids and then those guys came with a warrant and searched the car."

Stan said, "Must not have found anything or you'd be on the way up the river by now."

"Found nothing but frustration," said Jim.

Stan sniffed and observed, "Hmm. Your exhalations have an odd smell. Now, if I were Park Police I might be able to convince the U.S. Magistrate that I had probable cause for doing a more thorough search."

All three of us kept quiet.

"Times have changed fellows. Pressure is on, not just on you, on me too. I've only got a few years till retirement. I'm depending on it. Please don't put me or any of us in a bind. Can you understand what I'm saying? We have families. We don't want to have to make the hard choices, do you understand what I'm telling you?"

I said, "I understand."

Zack said, "We understand."

Jim said, "We'll put out the word. We know that things have changed. All we can do is try to preserve as much of the good time as possible, across this new time."

"Exactly," said Stan. "Maybe we can keep some of it alive. I doubt that it will ever get back to what it was."

"It is sort of sad, it was a special time, just couldn't last, world getting too complicated," I said.

"Exactly, fellows, go on," Stan told us, "and be careful, tell everyone to be careful, I don't think it's going to get better anytime soon."

We went on to Perry and Tim's. Tim was standing on the porch. "Hello, men, I see you made it past the Storm Troopers."

Zack said, "Yeah, close call, they searched my car."

Jim said, "Contingency Plan worked though, except for Bernie, got him with one roach."

"I heard. Too bad. Perry's inside on the phone, going to get Melvin Belli to represent him."

I'd heard that name, some kind of famous lawyer--good move, noble move.

"Come on in."

Tim offered us some lemonade and brownies. Perry joined us.

"Got that lined up. Belli says not to worry, Bernie will probably get off with 'time served' and probation."

"Still, he's going to have a criminal record," I mentioned, "and be handicapped by that for the rest of his life. Anyway, it is very noble of you to get him a good attorney. No telling what would happen if he just had some shyster."

"Like we've been telling you, Mike, we try to anticipate all contingencies and be ready for them," said Tim.

"I have to admit, it has been very impressive, seeing you all do things. I've learned a lot."

"We've learned from you, too, Mike."

I decided to announce to them that I would be leaving soon, headed back home, with bridge plans.

Tim seemed to have known and said, "Yes, it has come to that phase, you aren't the only one, dozens if not hundreds if not thousands, all getting back to where they once came from, all with plans to make it better."

I felt sad in a way. I was going to miss the mountains, the waterfalls, the Rangers and naturalists, the Hippies, the music and lights, the City... the drugs?...maybe...

I said, "Some of what I've learned out here I think I can make work back in Louisiana. Some of it won't work. I'll need to consult with all of you pretty often if you don't mind. There are going to be some rough spots in the road."

Tim said, "All our people, all our resources, it's all available to you, whatever we can do."

Perry asked, "What do you think won't work in Louisiana?"

"Mainly the drug element. Too dangerous, not just because of the laws, but no shepherds. Besides that, I know the way the scalawags think. They'd grab hold of it as a business idea, set up their own distribution network, use the money for their political purposes, become even more entrenched, look for ways to make it more and more lucrative, lock up supply, manipulate demand, carpetbaggers and scalawags have all that stuff perfected."

"So, that girder on the bridge has to have some substitute. Do you have anything in mind?" asked Tim.

I had nothing in mind. "It's a shame," I said. "The beauty it helps us see in the lights, in what we hear in the music, the truth it lays bare, none of that will be there to hold the bridge together. "

"Let us think about it, Mike."

Perry put on an album by a group called merely The Band. He said, "This group plays a tour circuit down where you come from, roadhouses mainly." They did have elements of old swamp pop rock and roll in their sound. A few years later one of their songs, Cripple Creek, would speak directly: "down in Lake Charles, Luziana…"

Later Zack and Jim gave me a ride to the summit trail head. I hiked up and spent the night with the Trail Crew. I thanked them for having helped Alain. I thought better about bringing up the Dunn incident. They didn't bring it up. I sensed that they were wondering if I would and that they were glad I didn't. Next morning I told them I was going to visit Dudley if I could find out where he'd been taken. They encouraged me to do that. I invited them to come down and visit me back home, anytime. Big Roy ceremonially gave me an axe. It was the one I'd learned how to throw. I realized that the Trail Crew was telling me that, even though I could never be on their level, I had at least attained something like being their little brother. "One more time, Mike, show us what you've learned!" I gave it a multidimensional fling and it split the bubble gum.

"Way to go, Mikey!" and hugs all around.

I walked down to the road and thumbed a ride into the Valley, surprised that anyone, even hippies would stop for someone with an axe. I said my goodbyes to Ranger Rick, told him to thank Naturalist Betty and the Superintendent and Ranger Anderson. Rick let me know that Dudley was in the VA psych ward in Phoenix.

I found Bob and Sara. She fed me something called tofu on whole wheat bread. It was edible.

It was a sad time in Yosemite. The season had changed. Winter was coming on.

Next day we left for the City. I retrieved the Turtle and told everyone I was going home.

I made my way to Arizona but after visiting Dudley who was thoroughly zonked out on Thorazine, I wrecked the Turtle and had to send its carcass to the crusher for recycling.

Epilogue

It is hard for me to get out the old albums and play them. I think that the last time was four or five years ago. When I hear those sounds I smile, and I grieve. I grieve for what was but then was lost. I grieve for what could have been but never quite happened. I smile because at least I knew that it was a special time, that I knew how privileged I was even at the time. I smile because I know that some of us made the most of something we knew could not last. We tried to make it last. We tried so hard...

I haven't been back to Yosemite, same reasons. I haven't tried to find Perry or Bob or Sara or Elena or Rick or any of the West Coast people I met... same reasons. There are too many good memories but too many dreams too late now to fulfill. I would not want to find all those people as let down as I have sometimes felt myself let down.

Maybe I would find them joyous and victorious. Would Sara and Jolie Blonde chastise the part of me they would call "Surrender Stuffington" or some clever but gentle put down? Would I find Zack, Jim, Perry, and Murphy still roaming Yosemite in the hearse, planning? Where is Elena? Maybe she is the mayor of Santa Cruz. Maybe if I went out there and got a prescription for some medical marijuana... Maybe I would really just stay next time...

I did go back to college and studied wetland ecology. It has been hard to make a living as a naturalist in Louisiana since the carpetbaggers and scalawags still manipulate almost everything including the main thing, the people. I've concentrated on reinforcing the efforts of neighborhood leaders who show the courage to stand up for their rights to have clean breathing air and safe drinking water. We've made the words "aquifer" and "hazardous wastes" familiar terms even beyond the State's borders. Louisiana has had numerous toxic waste site fights that we began long before Love Canal.

The politicians have tried, transparently, to co-opt our efforts but have underestimated the deep love of nature that has been passed from one renewable-resource-based generation to another. By giving voice and hope to the old ideals of self-sufficiency and harmony with nature we may have just in time halted what was almost a complete conversion of Louisiana into a depletable-resource-based economic and ecologic sacrifice zone, like a third world country right on the North American continent.

Now, finally, many of our citizens speak up vehemently on any issue. They are not afraid to be Americans exercising free speech. The carpetbaggers and scalawags are scrambling... but they are still in charge of and robbing what they know should be the richest state in the Union. Still, an unfinished bridge is unusable. Maybe someday Louisiana won't be a "sacrifice zone."

Alain sends me an e-mail every year with an update on his communal efforts near Cave Junction, Oregon, where he, Jolie Blonde, and Peyote Tom ended up.

Thaddeus's attempts to get the Wizards disciplined enough to succeed as musicians fell apart. Terry did become a studio musician in Los Angeles. Mongoose and Donnie still form and disband groups that play everything from zydeco to fusion, but they are getting old without hitting it big.

Thaddeus did become a state senator and did manage to get Alain a governor's pardon, just before the Governor managed to get himself into a federal prison for wiretapping the FBI. Sadly, Thaddeus, who had never smoked tobacco, died of lung cancer.

I, too, never having smoked tobacco, have developed chronic obstructive pulmonary disease, COPD, usually reserved for tobacco smokers. In my situation I am convinced that the stretching of the air sacs happened during the times that the hashish smoke expanded within my lungs. Maybe that is why Middle-Easterners invented hookahs, to allow expansion prior to the hot vapor reaching the alveoli. It is too bad that our society is so uptight that it cannot do truly pertinent research into the adverse and beneficial effects of any drug and then provide warnings that people would believe instead of disregarding as "establishment propaganda." To me it is complete hypocrisy for our society to allow nicotine and alcohol while preaching that marijuana inevitably leads to hard drugs like cocaine and heroin. Of all the Louisiana people I have kept up with from my time in the sixties, not one of those people went on to cocaine, heroin, or methamphetamine. Terry did become an alcoholic. Mongoose did become addicted to nicotine. Most of the church people I know drink coffee. Drugs are drugs.

Kenny finally showed himself to be a born scalawag. He is now a millionaire attorney representing primarily carpetbaggers who continue to suppress Louisiana's educational system so that labor will be cheap and desperate, so that environmental regulations can be circumvented, so that Reconstruction can continue.

William has been in and out of jail, including a misdemeanor bust for agitating in Ohio, just before the Kent State shootings. He took the "turn 'em on and turn 'em loose" mission, without shepherding, all across the South. I still don't know what was so funny about the Jefferson Airplane having given him a sheepskin coat. I always forgot to ask because some of his other chaos overrode the conversations. I still pray for him.

Nathan and Marnie married and are happy, nearing retirement in San Francisco. Nathan, with a single phone call to his Dad back home, set into motion the plan to have a new marshal then become the new sheriff. The parish, with term limits now in effect, is on its third new sheriff. That is another bridge that worked.

Alexis lost her home in the Katrina flood, plans to rebuild, will lose that one too, and, as a shrink now has to deal with the overload of traumatized people still in Orleans denial. Deathtrap denial trying to heal deathtrap denial, it is maddening.

I tried to build a "bridge" that would have saved New Orleans. I think that my failure to build that "bridge," the concept that would have relocated the city to high ground north of Lake Pontchartrain, is the greatest grief I have. To have known what was going to happen, to have come home and spoken in so many public hearings, written so many comment letters, submitted to the Office of State Planning an actual budget for the relocation, only to have everyone except my ecology professors laugh at the thought of relocating a whole city to save it... and now to see that the lesson has not been learned... Orleans Denial/Deathtrap Blues...that is the greatest grief. I do not know how I will be able to stand it when they drown another set of children.

The Creator has allowed me to have many great moments since I left California, enough to have kept me going, to have kept hope from being fully extinguished. There are, at least, public hearings, and, the public does have the courage now to attend and often even speak up against the scalawags and carpetbaggers. Yet, I look up at night and the stars, though still there, are dimmed by our thick, polluted humidity, dimmed by the loss of what could have been.

We have had heroes and we have had horrors.

Yes, only a few of my bridges came to any tangible completion. I look across the country and get the impression that everyone else's dream bridges have also been delayed, at least. I look back and think that "The Revolution" was more like an ejaculation, its seeds smothered by a fearful society's prophylactic inertia, the same inertia that is still killing America. I would like to see some new generation prove me wrong.

I struggle to believe that the Creator might again allow some new generation to flower, to experience that special time of love, peace, and a sense of regaining power. I still look forward to hearing the songs that never made it onto the stage or into the albums. I want to believe and hope. I make myself believe and hope but I really need another hit of fresh air.

Sometimes I let myself dream that even my lost wraithgirl will be waiting somewhere for me. By the moonlight maybe we can fly and glide in and around and over the bridge supports and from star to star. Maybe we will see you looking up with hopes, dreams, and plans.

One more ride in the hearse and I will finally be back home.

About the Author:

Michael Tritico is a retired biologist, a former naturalist, who now lives alone in rural Louisiana. He provides technical assistance to leaders of neighborhoods experiencing public health and environmental problems. With other environmental advocates he presses for restoration of explicit symmetry to our ravaged earth (RESTORE), or as he says in other words: "Put it back the way the Creator had it, because He had it right." Michael believes that the Supreme Consciousness expects us to stand up for the dynamic equilibrium that, if not distorted by the forces of evil, would not just sustain all forms of existing life in pleasant harmony but would allow creation of so-far-unimagined forms of self-reproducing beauty.